NO
is not enough

Helping Teenagers Avoid Sexual Assault

Caren Adams, Jennifer Fay & Jan Loreen-Martin

Impact **Publishers**

SAN LUIS OBISPO, CALIFORNIA

Fifth Printing, September, 1990

Library of Congress Cataloging in Publication Data
Adams, Caren, 1946-
        No is not enough.

        1. Sex instruction.   2. Rape — Prevention.
3. Youth — Crimes against.   I. Fay, Jennifer, 1949-
1949-   II. Loreen-Martin, Jan, 1947-
III. Title.
HQ57.A33   1984   306.7'7   84-20506
ISBN 0-915166-35-6 [pbk.]

Cover design and illustration by Joe Boddy, Missoula,
Montana.

Printed in the United States of America.

Published by **Impact ⟘ Publishers**
POST OFFICE BOX 1094
SAN LUIS OBISPO, CALIFORNIA 93406

Contents

Dedication

To our children, Toby, Piper, Ginevra and Gregory, and to all the other children and parents who have the right to grow up in a world free of sexual violence.

Acknowledgements

The authors wish to thank Suzanne Ageton, Cordelia Anderson, Walter Andrews, Lucy Berliner, Julia A. Boyd, Scott Dills, Ann Downer, David Finkelhor, Billie Jo Flerchinger, Marie M. Fortune, Karen Hausrath, Caren Monastersky, Ruth Montgomery, Millie Mullarky, Beth Reis, Diana E.H. Russell, Tony Silvestrin, Dee Smiley, and Wileen Toperosky for sharing their expertise and for their helpful suggestions and support.

A special thanks to the parents who contributed their stories and concern, and to Herb, Robbie and Billy.

Caren Adams, Jennifer Fay, Jan Loreen-Martin

Introduction

"I started talking about sexual abuse with my children when they were little. We talked about good touches, bad touches, and touches that were confusing. And we talked about what to do. I told them they could say 'no', that their bodies belonged to them and they could decide who touched them. My children know that they can tell me when someone older asks them to keep a secret and that it's not their fault if someone tries to abuse them — that the adult should know better.
But now my children are older — 11 and 13. They are out on their own much more with other kids. They are almost old enough to start dating, and I know sexual assaults can happen in a dating situation. I know it's no longer helpful just to say, 'Don't let anyone touch you in a way that's uncomfortable' — they need so much more than that. What can I tell my older kids — teenagers, really — about sexual assault?"

This book is for parents, to help in talking with teenagers about sexual assault. It is written both for those parents who have been talking with their kids about sexual assault since the kids were little, and for parents who haven't known what to say, but also are concerned about sexual assault. Parents *can* help protect teenagers from sexual assault and exploitation, and this book tells how. We also hope to help change the attitudes which perpetuate sexual violence in our society.

All parents worry that their teens will make mistakes, be hurt, or be taken advantage of while exploring relationships and sexuality. Many parents are also concerned that their children may take advantage of or hurt others.

The traditional approach parents have taken regarding sexual assault is to warn their teenagers:

- Don't hitchhike
- Don't let anyone into the house when we aren't home
- Don't go out alone at night

These warnings can be helpful, but they don't go far enough. They are focused on strangers, when *over half of all reported rapes of teens are by acquaintances.*

Most children are sexually assaulted by someone they know — not by a stranger. There is an awareness among parents today that sexual assault and exploitation happen frequently. Yet studies show that most parents don't say any more than "Don't get any girls in trouble," or "Be careful." We teach our daughters to say "no" to sexual intercourse — and we say hardly anything at all to our sons.

But "no" is not enough. It isn't enough to stop teens from becoming victims of sexual assault, or to stop them from becoming victimizers.

To avoid being exploited, abused, or pushed into sexual contact before they are ready, teens need enough information to be able to recognize when those situations are developing, and tools to resist the pressures. They need to know *what to do.*

Parents may ask themselves: Which do we do? Talk with our daughters about how to protect themselves from sexual assault, or talk to our sons about changing male behavior so that things will change for our daughters? The answer is that *both* are needed to protect our children from sexual abuse, and to begin to change the conditions which perpetuate sexual violence.

> **AVOIDING SEXUAL ASSAULT AND EXPLOITATION TAKES:**
> - knowing what sexual assault is
> - knowing what to do if it happens
> - knowing that it's okay to talk about the negative and positive sides of sexuality
> - knowing that rape is never deserved
> - knowing that values should limit our sexual behavior and that force is never justified

Talking about sexual assault is never easy. With teens it can be even harder:

- Teens are separating from their parents and questioning parental values and ideas.
- Many parents lack information and are unsure what to say about acquaintance rape and other kinds of sexual exploitation.
- Some parents may have been sexually assaulted and find it a particularly painful subject.
- Many parents haven't talked with their kids much about sexuality yet and don't want to start with the negative side. They may be afraid they will warp their teens' developing sexuality, cause them to unfairly mistrust others, or "put ideas into their heads."
- Teens often are uncomfortable when parents bring it up: "Oh, Mom, I know all that stuff!"

Keeping our fingers crossed and hoping that they don't get hurt will not protect our kids. They need *information* and *skills*. Teenagers without information about sexual assault are much more vulnerable than they need to be.

Sexual assault is often discussed as though it were unrelated to sexuality. In fact, the two are closely linked. Violence is considered by many to be sexy, and sex often includes violence. Some of what is accepted as normal sexual behavior actually includes some forms of sexual assault.

Talking about sexual assault makes the most sense in the context of talking about a range of sexual behavior. Teens need to understand the difference between healthy sexuality and abusiveness and exploitation. The difference between rape, sexual exploitation and consenting sex is how much, and what kind of pressure and/or force is used. Teens are eager for that information, especially if a discussion of values, morals and the emotions that surround sex goes along with it.

Why A Book For Parents?

Parents are in the best position to talk to kids about sexual assault, to provide help to their teens and to structure this information to be consistent with family values and rules.

We've tried to make this book as practical as possible. We are parents too, and we know there isn't always as much time as we would like to talk to our children. We don't expect any parent to use *all* this information. Our hope is that readers will pick and choose ideas which might work for their families.

We would like to be able to say that we have easy answers that will completely protect teens from sexual assault; that if you tell them, for example, to be assertive, to say no, to get angry and fight back that they will never encounter sexual assault or exploitation. But such easy answers do not exist.

This book is not meant to add to the burden of sexual assault victims. When people are not able to protect themselves, a sexual assault is no more their fault than when people do protect themselves.

Even if you think your teenager will never experience sexual violence in any form, it is important that all teens know what sexual assault is, what to do if it happens and why it happens.

Our teens will be safer when all parents — of both boys and girls — take on the task of lessening sexual violence in our society. Only then can we hope to prevent and eventually eliminate sexual violence from our lives.

Chapter 1

"What Teens Don't Know Can Hurt Them"

Parents and other adults usually have definite ideas about what teenagers are like. To adults, teens seem to:

- see things in black or white, right or wrong (People are neat or they're creeps.)
- act like they "know it all"
- lack self-esteem
- need to be "cool"
- be vulnerable to peer pressure
- not see adults as credible
- have limited knowledge of the world
- fear ridicule, or not being popular
- take risks
- test limits and challenge rules, pushing for independence
- feel invincible, immortal
- act in intense, extreme ways. (Things can be a massive crisis or no big deal.)
- act adult one day and child-like the next.

Any of these typical teen qualities can play a part in making a teen vulnerable to exploitation. But most teens have additional attitudes which increase their vulnerability:

- they don't know what sexual assault is

"That guy in the movie came on real strong and she loved it."

"Why would a prostitute mind being raped?"

"I've done it sometimes when I didn't want to, but I've never been raped."

- they need and want to take risks, to push the limits on sexual behavior

    "I never thought it could happen to me. I just went to the party to have some fun."

- they have misconceptions about why and how rape happens

    "I wouldn't let that happen to me."

    "She must have let him do it. Anyone can stop rape if they really want to."

    "Rape happens mostly to 'bad' girls."

    "What did she expect, being out alone late at night?"

    "What did she think would happen wearing those clothes?"

    "She got him all excited and led him on. What was he supposed to do?"

"But he's such a nice boy. It couldn't be true."

"You have to be mentally ill to rape someone."

"If a rapist attacked me, I'd kill him."

- they are confused and embarrassed about sexuality

    "I could never tell my parents if I were assaulted. They would die."

    "Is rape like sex?"

    "Am I normal if I think about raping someone?"

    "Am I normal if I don't want sex?"

    "If sex is supposed to be so great, then how come this seems so crummy?"

- they are bombarded with conflicting messages from the media, their peers, and the community about sex and violence

    "How come women like to be raped in some of these shows?"

    "Do you think women can really fall in love with a guy who raped them?"

"Lucy's brother says that once a boy is turned on he can't stop, so girls better watch out."

"Have you heard about the latest craze in makeup? It makes your face look black and blue, like someone has beaten you up."

Teenagers are working at becoming independent and experimenting with relationships and sexuality. They take risks and test their ability to cope with the outside world. They challenge parental rules and test their limits, pushing away from their parents in order to gain independence. But when they have pushed too far, gotten scared or hurt, they still need to rely on parental protection. Teens lead a push-pull life.

So do their parents. It is the job of parents of teens to let them go, to trust them, to help them venture out, and — when they are "in over their heads" — to bail them out. With both parents and teens pushing and pulling, it is inevitable that disagreements arise, especially differences about situations which may be sexually risky.

Kids want to expand the limits of activity. Parents don't always know what they want for their children, or what to say. Many parents don't want to repeat the repressive message given by *their* parents, which was usually some variation on, "Sex is forbidden till you are married, then it is suddenly okay." Nor do parents want to say "Well, go ahead and do whatever feels good." The result is that many parents say nothing at all on the subject. At the time in their lives when teens are actively deciding on their own views and values about sexuality, they may get little information from their parents.

It is hard to make good choices when there is limited knowledge on which to base them. Fewer than 10% of teens nationally receive comprehensive sex education in school.

Source: Sex Information and Education Council of the United States.

Risk taking behavior also makes teens vulnerable. In many cases of teen rape, for example, the girl has been doing something her parents wouldn't approve of: hitchhiking, smoking dope, drinking, sneaking out, running away, breaking a rule, letting a friend in the house when no one is home, taking a dare. Teens may also believe that since they broke a rule, the rape was somehow "deserved."

The following story of acquaintance rape is typical: Sandy broke some rules, and felt trapped by the situation.

Sandy's parents were out of town, so she was spending the night with her friend Julie, who lives across from the high school.

They made a plan to sneak out and meet their boyfriends at school after midnight. Sandy was hesitant about sneaking out, but it seemed exciting and she had never done it before.

Being with the guys was fun — meeting secretly, horsing around, kissing a little. After a while Julie got nervous and wanted to go home — but Sandy wanted to stay a bit longer with her boyfriend, John. Julie went home by herself.

When Sandy decided to go in she tapped on the bedroom window, but couldn't wake Julie. She thought knocking at the door would wake Julie's parents, and she didn't want to get Julie or herself in trouble. Then her boyfriend John said, "Why don't you go to your house. I know your parents aren't home but you have a key, don't you? I'll walk you home, 'cause it wouldn't be safe for you alone at night."

When they got to Sandy's house, she told John goodnight and that she'd talk to him tomorrow. "Couldn't I come in just for minute, just to rest? I still have a long walk home, you know?" John said.

Sandy thought he was nice to bring her home, but didn't want to let him in when her parents weren't there. She was feeling pressured. She said "No, I'm sorry, you'll have to leave." He continued to pressure her. "What's the matter, don't you trust me? Couldn't I come in and get just a drink of water?" Sandy was feeling confused. How could she tell him she was not sure she trusted him? She didn't want to hurt his feelings. He was so nice to walk her all the way home just so she could be safe. How could she refuse him a drink? "Okay, you can come in just for a minute, just to get a drink."

They talked for a little longer. John didn't try anything, but she felt uncomfortable. Sandy told him, "You had better go now." "Only after a kiss," he replied. Oh no, Sandy thought, I'll never get him out of the house. He won't listen to me. "Just one kiss," she said, "then will you go?" But when she kissed him, he wouldn't let go, and that is when it happened.

He pushed her down on the couch. She struggled, but John was a lot bigger and stronger. She was on her back, pinned down. Sandy couldn't believe this was happening to her. She thought about reaching for the huge ashtray on the coffee table and hitting him over the head. She thought, what if I split open his head — what if it makes him so angry that he hurts me worse? What if I knock him unconscious? Who would I call — what would I say? "Help, I just hurt this guy I know, who I let into my house when my parents weren't home. I sneaked out with him from my friend's house in the middle of the night and he tried to rape me?" Who would believe that?

Sandy fought hard, but she was pinned down, trapped. John thought it was a great date and he is feeling good about himself. He scored.

John needed to prove himself, to prove he could make a conquest. He is thinking only about himself.

Sandy can't believe this has happened. She is feeling terrible.

She was raped.

From *Top Secret: Sexual Assault Information For Teenagers Only* by Jennifer Fay and Billie Jo Flerchinger. Copyright © 1983 by King County Rape Relief. Used with permission.

A survey of Minneapolis public high school students indicated that teenagers generally understand on an emotional level what it must "feel" like to be a victim of a rape or sexual abuse, or what it may "feel" like to be an abuser. However, the same survey also revealed that many teens feel sexual abuse can be the victim's fault, and that some teens believe that their parents' only reaction to sexual abuse would be to blame the teen for what happened.

A survey of sexually active girls 16 and under found that what they most wanted information on was how to say no without hurting the other person's feelings.

Most teens are confused about the difference between healthy sexual expression and exploitation or abuse. Their apparent sophistication about sex is often only a veneer.

Knowledge about sex is sought after from parents, peers, books, movies, magazines and the like. Children and adolescents usually gain a mass of confused information through this process. They also acquire "healthy" or "unhealthy" attitudes and feelings about male and female sexuality. Males are less likely than females to receive sex information from their parents and teachers because girls are thought to be more in need of knowledge that can protect them. This creates particular problems for boys, because they are socialized to think they should be more expert on the topic of sex than girls.

From *Adolescent Sexuality in a Changing Society.* Catherine S. Chilman. New York: John Wiley and Sons, 1983.

Experts agree that most of today's teens actually know very little about their bodies and their developing sexuality. Teens often act as if they "know it all," but it is only an act. It is especially important for teens, particularly boys, to appear to be knowledgeable.

Most of what teenagers know about sexual assault comes from stories they hear from their friends or the media. They think mainly in terms of guns, knives, strangers and weirdos. Very few understand what sexual assault is, why it happens (they feel that some victims must have asked for it), and why it is wrong (it happens so much, it can't be that big a deal, can it?).

As a result, many teens accept abusive, exploitive behavior because they don't know any better or don't know how to change things. Sexuality education experts are concerned that most teenage "groping" and other sexual exploration is mutually exploitive. Research indicates that many sexually active teens do not enjoy their sexual experiences, yet they lack the knowledge and family support to change their relationships.

> When some college age men were asked if they would rape a woman if they knew they wouldn't be caught and punished, 51% of the men said they might.
> The men also indicated that they thought the victim would enjoy it.
>
> From Seymour Feshbach and Neil Malamuth, "Sex and Aggression." *Psychology Today*, November 1978.

Teenagers also have many sexual misunderstandings. They are unaware of how different it is to grow up male or grow up female.

"My daughter and her friends kept complaining about the bra-snapping that the boys in her class do. Her teacher decided to have a class discussion. After the girls told the boys they didn't like it, the boys said, 'If you don't like it, why do you laugh and giggle?' The girls said, 'Because we are so embarrassed, ...we don't know what else to do.' The boys were surprised. They really thought the girls liked it. The bra snapping stopped after that."

What teenagers don't know about sexual assault can hurt them. Their lack of information leaves them much more vulnerable than they need to be. When teens know:
- offenders can be someone they know
- sexual assaults happen in everyday life
- the force is likely to be trickery or deception
- offenders will try to put the blame on them
- pressuring or tricking someone into sex is never okay
- they will get help if they tell
- taking care of themselves means setting limits, not letting people pressure them, and listening to their own feelings

they will be much more able to protect themselves and much more likely to build a world that finds sexual assault intolerable.

Keep In Mind

- Teens want and need to know more about sex and sexual assault, yet are unlikely to ask.
- They have heard a lot about sexual issues and sexual assault, and have many misconceptions.
- They are likely to follow parental guidelines about behavior if they know what the guidelines are.

Chapter 2

Acquaintance Rape and Sexual Exploitation: What Really Happens?

The word rape brings to mind images of teenagers being violently attacked while hitchhiking, or while walking city streets late at night. It's hard to imagine anyone who's violently attacked preventing that assault. But most sexual assaults of teenagers don't happen that way. *Teens are most likely to be sexually assaulted by an acquaintance* — at home, at a friend's home or in a car. Acquaintance rape and child sexual assault are the two forms of sexual assault that teens face most often.

What We Fear	*What Is More Likely To Happen: Child Sexual Assault*	*What Is More Likely To Happen: Acquaintance Rape*
Dangerous weird stranger	A person the child knows and trusts who is older and has some authority: father, stepfather, grandfather or someone else in the parenting role: teacher, neighbor, babysitter, coach.	A person known and trusted, often close in age: boyfriend, friend of a friend, someone just met, the local store clerk, someone known at school, a neighbor.
Violent attack	Bribery and threats rather than extreme physical force: "This is our secret." "If you tell, you'll go to jail." "I'm doing this because I love you."	Threats of or actual physical force, pushing, shoving, grabbing arms or wrists, holding down, hitting, slapping, or other threats of harm or threats of harm to others. The force in sexual exploitation is deception, manipulation, pressure. "'I won't be your friend anymore." "I won't like you anymore." "I'll tell everybody that you did anyway."

Out of the blue, surprise	A situation that develops gradually over a period of time, usually starting when the child was younger.	Develops gradually, over a period of time. Teens are likely to ignore feelings that "something isn't right" and assume they've misinterpreted the offender's behavior. "I asked for it." "I gave him the wrong idea." "I should have known better."
Isolated extreme incident	Frequent incidents, taking many forms. Most likely to be sexual contact other than intercourse. May involve other family members. May go on for years. Boys are victims too, about as often as girls. Disclosures of abuse often occur at puberty.	More often a one time attack, usually not reported and wrongly considered less harmful than stranger rape. Not taken seriously often because "nice boys" are involved. Rape means forced sexual intercourse; (the legal definition includes oral sexual contact and penetration of anus or vagina by penis or object).

The full extent of acquaintance rape and exploitation is not known. Even acquaintance rape with obvious force is rarely reported. Assaults achieved through deception or trickery are even less likely to be talked about, and least likely to be reported to the authorities, or anyone else.

Conservative estimates are that one in four girls and one in ten boys experience sexual assault as they grow up. Boys are more likely to be victimized by child sexual assault or sexual exploitation than by acquaintance rape.

The likelihood of teens telling they have been raped is small. Most feel they won't be believed or taken seriously, or fear they will get into trouble or be blamed. Many are not sure what happened to them and question whether it is rape if they knew the guy, and agreed to be with him.

What Is the Impact? How Does Rape Affect A Teenager?

Although the tendency for both the teen and parent may be to underestimate the possible effects of forced sexual contact from someone known, its impact can be severe. Even when teenage victims realize they have been forced, they may not label what happened as rape. Many victims confuse their own submission (out of fear, guilt, or confusion) with consent.

Social isolation, bad feelings about themselves, an inability to concentrate, difficulties in school and difficulty trusting others are possible effects. These difficulties in school and with friends can create severe problems for teens that aren't easily handled by the teenager, his or her family, or the community.

Sexual assault may be a factor in causing much troubled teenaged behavior. Many teens involved in running away, prostitution, drug abuse, or suicide have been victims of sexual assault. The severity of the effects increases the importance of finding ways to help teens avoid acquaintance rape and child sexual assault.

Who Assaults?

The hardest part for teens to understand is that the person who victimizes teenagers is most often someone known to them. Every teen is convinced that all they need to do is look out for the crazy guy, the weirdo. And teens are sure that no one they know would ever do anything like that. But, sexual offenders are usually not crazy in any way which shows, other than their willingness to use force. They may be "successful," charming, and well-liked. They may show anger when they don't get their way. Some are self-centered, "me"-oriented people. They have no sense that the needs of the other person should be considered. Of course, teens who use more "acceptable" forms of pressure for sexual contact may not show even these characteristics.

Although the offenders in acquaintance rape and sexual exploitation are almost always male, women are involved in some child sexual assault and sexual exploitation. The adult man and younger teen girl as a romantic couple is so common it almost goes unnoticed, but it is still sexual exploitation based on their inequality in experience and power. In the same way, the adult woman/teen boy couple is exploitive.

The Situation

Teens are taken advantage of, exploited and raped in every day situations: dating, at friends' houses, partying, breaking rules, going to school and trying to find a job. They can be taken advantage of and trapped because of:

- their fear of getting into trouble
- their inexperience and lack of information about
  sexuality
- their need and the outside pressure to enter the
  world of love and romance
- the sheer numbers of new people in their lives
- their trust of others and their willingness to
  think they have misunderstood another's intentions
- their belief that if they are good, good things
  will happen to them, if bad things happen, they
  must have deserved it.

The Force

Teens may well have heard that rape is a violent, not a
sexual crime. But, teens are more likely to encounter rape in
situations of sexual bargaining rather that in interactions
which seem violent. They are most likely to be up against
verbal pressure. In acquaintance rape, verbal pressure may
be followed by grabbing or shoving.

The difference between rape, sexual exploitation and
consenting sex is how much, and what kind of pressure and
force is used.

Parents may find the following continuum a useful
starting point for thinking about consent, and for talking with
their teens about the differences between consenting sex,
exploitation and rape. These behaviors blend into each other,
making it difficult to know where one begins and the other
ends. This continuum ranges from *consent*, through
increasing *coercion*, to *violence*. Because teens are learning
and experimenting with sexual behavior, they are more likely
to be confused about the ways people make decisions about
sex, are pressured into sex, and are forced. A continuum from
freely consenting to stranger rape might look like this:

FORCE CONTINUUM

1——2——3——4——5——6——7——8

1. Freely consenting   5. Silent Rape
  2. Filling the other's needs   6. Bribery or coercion
    3. Economic partnership   7. Acquaintance rape
     4. Seduction   8. Stranger rape

1. Only partners with equal power can *freely consent*.
   Equal power means partners have equal knowledge and
   economic status, and are of similar ages. Although no
   partners are exactly equal in all areas, there needs to be a
   balance approaching evenness.

   In child sexual assault there is no issue of consent. It
   is not up to children to consent or not consent to sexual
   contact with adults. Children are not capable of such a
   decision. For teens, especially of similar ages, consent
   needs to be defined. In nearly all states the law defines
   the age of consent as 16, because society agrees that
   people younger than that don't have adequate experience
   and knowledge to give consent.

2. When one partner agrees to have sex in order *to
   fulfill the other's needs*, although he or she may not
   be as interested in sex at the moment, it is still
   consent if they are equal partners.

3. *Economic partnership* exists when one person provides
   sex as part of a partnership agreement. In the past, women
   were not expected to like sex, but were expected to go
   along with it as part of marriage. However if force is
   used, even within marriage, it becomes non-consenting
   sex.

Prostitution is also an economic bargain. Consent may be considered present if there is not physical violence, and the prostitute is of age. It is child sexual assault if a child below the age of consent enters into a prostitution agreement, despite the economic bargain.

4. *Seduction* means one person tries to persuade the other person to have sex. When considering consent, the question becomes, "What kind of persuasion is used?" The seduction is positive if it is a genuine, friendly, gentle show of feelings. The other person may not use words, but music, lighting, or small gifts. It is not seduction if force, bribery, or emotional blackmail is used.

5. *Silent rape* occurs if one partner gives in and has sex for fear of potential violence if she/he resists. Although there may be no obvious threat, the victim senses a willingness on the other's part to use violence, and therefore decides "to go along" with the sex, rather than experience the powerlessness of being forced. Although this is not legally rape, true consent is not present.

6. *Bribery or coercion* involves emotional and psychological force. It is often used in relationships of unequal power. The bribery or coercion may be an extension of the natural authority one partner has over the other. A counselor who says to a client, "It will be good for you." is abusing the client's trust to gain sexual contact. An adult who gets a teen to go along with sexual activity simply by telling the teen to is using adult authority. A neighbor who says, "I'll let you ride my motorcycles if you pose for pictures nude," is using both adult authority and bribery.

7. *Acquaintance rape* occurs when the trust of a relationship is used to get another into a powerless or defenseless position. An example is the story of Sandy in Chapter 1, in her own house when no one was home. It is rape when force or threats are used to gain sexual contact.

8. *Stranger rape* is the most obviously forced non-consenting sexual contact. Stranger rape almost always involves threatened or actual physical violence.

Rape is puzzling. In one context the physical act is loving and affectionate, and in another, it is one of the most painful, destructive things one human can do to another. Between those two extremes are many puzzling uses of sex. Talking about this range of behavior can answer the question many kids ask, "Is rape like sex?" and may help teens better understand the difference between taking advantage of each other and taking care with each other.

Teens are better able to avoid an assault when they realize:
- it may be a friend, or date, who might use unfair and hurtful methods to gain sexual contact
- sexual assault is most likely to happen in situations that seem safe
- the difference between okay, positive, healthy sexual contact and rape is not the sexual contact, but the force.

Chapter 3

Talking With Teenagers About Acquaintance Rape

Parents want to protect their teens so much they sometimes use scare tactics to get them to listen. Because teenagers believe they can take care of themselves and want to be thought of as capable, they're unlikely to believe anything bad would happen to them. However, few teens really understand acquaintance rape or sexual assault, how it happens, who might do it, or what they can realistically do to protect themselves. Teens need more than "Be careful," "Don't take advantage," "Don't trust." They can only protect themselves when they know clearly what it is that might happen.

Getting Started

• *Decide on your own definition of rape.* If you defined sexual assault for your children when they were younger as an invasion of privacy, or unwanted, uncomfortable touch, or said, "No one should touch your private parts," that's your starting point. A definition for teens might be "Rape is someone holding another down and forcing sexual intercourse." Or "Sexual assault is someone tricking another into sexual activity." "Sexual exploitation is when someone uses deception or bribery to gain sexual contact with another."

There are three aspects of how sexual assaults happen which teens need to understand:

WHO: Teens are still expecting a stranger. Parents' hardest task will be helping them understand a sexual assault would most likely be committed by someone they *know*.

FORCE: Teens may have fantasies of how they could physically resist: ''I'd kill the guy first.'' Parents need to help teens realize the force most likely to be used is much more subtle, and that they are unlikely to respond with physical force to someone they know.

SITUATION: Teens expect rape to happen as a sudden surprise attack. The parent's task is to show how it is more likely to happen during the normal course of school and social activities. The situation is more complicated than with younger kids. Because sexual exploration is part of normal activity for teenagers, it is no longer enough to talk about not letting someone touch your private parts, or about uncomfortable or confusing touch. Most touching that happens on a date or with a group of kids may feel confusing to them. They are unlikely to say ''no'' and go tell someone.

• *Think ahead about how to deal with discomfort, both yours and your teenager's.*

EMPHASIZE your desire to be helpful. Resolve not to use scare tactics.

*"Our rules are our attempt to protect you. If they
don't work, we still want to help. I'm worried about
acquaintance rape. I want to help you avoid it."*

PRESENT ideas as those you wish you had known when
you were a teen.

*"When I was growing up, my parents didn't talk about
rape. They wanted to help, they just didn't know how.
I wish I had known that it's still rape, even if you
know the guy."*

*"When I was growing up the only thing my father said
to me about how to treat girls was, 'Don't take
advantage of them.' He was trying to be helpful but
I didn't know what he meant. What does taking
advantage of a girl mean to you?"*

ACCEPT vague answers rather than pressing for details.
Asking for details can sound like an interrogation.

LISTEN to the answers. Sometimes everybody is in such a
hurry to talk, no one listens.

TIME your discussions. The teen getting ready to go out
on a date is unlikely to listen if this is the first conversation
about acquaintance rape. It may seem that you are only
concerned about this person. Loyalty to their dates will keep
teens from understanding that what is being said applies to
anytime they go out with anyone. Teens will listen better at a
more neutral time — shopping together, lunch, making
dinner.

PREPARE for responding in a way that keeps communication going.

> *"When my son, just home from a date, asked if I thought a girl 'owed' a guy sex because he had spent money on her, it was all I could do to keep from falling apart. I knew that wouldn't help, so I made myself a cup of tea and thought about my answer. When the tea was made, I was able to talk with him without losing my cool. I'll use that the next time — give myself a moment before I jump into a heavy discussion."*

FOLLOW the five sentence rule. Anything a parent needs to say can be said in five sentences. After that ideas are either being repeated or a new idea should be introduced.

Conversation Starters

Athough there are many ways to start a conversation, the easiest is to ask about what your teens already know.

> *"I'm sure you get lots of information at school [church, other groups]. But I'm not sure what they tell you. Could you fill me in a little?"*

This also helps parents identify the myths and misinformation their child already believes.

> *"Have you ever had speakers at school about date rape, incest, or child abuse?*
>
> *"What's the scariest thing about going out on a first date with someone?"*

"I know you'd rather I didn't worry about you but I do. Have you thought about what you would do if someone you dated started to act like he or she didn't care what you wanted?"

"That movie showed a girl who liked being slapped around. Do you think the girl liked it?"

"That song says, 'Violent sex. I want violent sex.' What does that mean?"

If nothing else seems to work, and your teenager won't respond to any of your concerns, try:

"All right, it probably won't happen to you but just for my peace of mind, can we talk about what you might do if... [give specific examples]... happens?"

Once you've started communication you can ask questions about the situations they face. For instance, parents need to know what ideas about force their teens already have.

"Do you and your friends ever worry about being forced to have sex with a guy? Do your friends think it is okay for a guy to use pressure to get sex? When might it be all right to use more than that?"

A parent might explain acquaintance rape or sexual exploitation by saying:

"Acquaintance rape is when a guy holds a girl down and forces his penis in her vagina."
(For younger teens an anatomical explanation may be most useful).

With older teens there is less need to be specific and more examples about the forms of assault can be added:

"It's when someone like a date or a friend pressures or pushes you to do more sexually than you wanted to do."

"Acquaintance rape is when a guy forces a girl to have sex with him. That might include oral sex or other kinds of sexual contact."

Here's one way to describe how acquaintance rape might happen:

"The guy can get close to her because she trusts him and doesn't want to think badly of him, or because she wants him to like her."

"The guy thinks he won't get into trouble. He counts on her to not make trouble. He figures she'll share the blame or feel as if she asked for it, and not tell anyone."

The force that is used might be explained this way:

- someone who tries to make you feel bad:

  "What's the matter, don't you like me?"

  "Don't tell me you're afraid of me."

- someone who pressures for sex:

  "You're not the only girl I could date."

> *"If you loved me, you would."*

> *"If you don't I'll tell the guys you did anyway."*

- someone who does not take "no" for an answer:

> *"What do you mean 'no'? I spent all that money on you!"*

> *"You really want it. You're just saying 'no' to protect your reputation; girls are supposed to do that."*

- someone who feels sex is his right:

> *"You led me on."*

> *"You've turned me on. Now you have to do it."*

> *"We've had sex before; you can't say 'no' now."*

- someone who uses emotional blackmail:

> *"I'll kill myself if you break up with me."*

Parents want teens to be able to choose based on their own values, and not be pressured, forced, or exploited.

> *Consent is based on choice. Consent is active, not*
> *passive. Consent is possible only when there is*
> *equal power. Giving in because of fear is not*
> *consent. Going along with something because of*
> *wanting to fit in with the group, being deceived*
> *or feeling bad is not consent. If you can't say*
> *'no' comfortably, then 'yes' has no meaning. If*
> *you are unwilling to accept a 'no,' then 'yes'*
> *has no meaning.*

Detailed Examples

Occasionally parents will be able to spend longer talking.
Giving teens specific examples may help them see parents'
concerns. Many teens under 15 don't generalize well; they are
still developing their ability to understand abstractions.
Stories can help.

A good place to start is with general stories.

> *"When a guy takes a girl out, he wants the girl*
> *to pay attention to him, not everybody else.*
> *Sometimes a girl will go out with a guy just to go*
> *out. But when they get around other guys, she flirts*
> *with them. The guy she went out with may feel angry*
> *or bad. What would you do if a girl did that to you?"*

While this is not sexual exploitation, it is a common
dating problem. Boys need to be taught how to deal with
feeling rejected and angry. One way might be to help boys
find acceptable ways to express their feelings and hurts. Or
start a conversation by asking, "How do you handle rejection?

Do you pretend it's no big deal? Do you tell yourself you
didn't like her in the first place?''

> *"I always looked forward to summer camp. It was*
> *a great place to get to know other kids and experiment*
> *a little. One year one of my friends went further*
> *sexually with a boy there than she would have with*
> *someone from home. He promised he would be her*
> *boyfriend and wouldn't tell anyone. She thought*
> *he meant it. But he had friends who went to our school.*
> *When school started she heard rumors about herself,*
> *and that her 'boyfriend' had gone back to his old*
> *girlfriend. I remember how hurt she was..."*

Such a recollection helps personalize your concern, and
points out that when someone lies to get sexual contact with
another, that is sexual exploitation.

> *"I remember a party that I went to when I was*
> *your age. There was a guy there that I didn't*
> *know, but some of the other kids did. He seemed*
> *interested in me. He came over to me and stood*
> *really close, as if he knew me well, and leaned*
> *so close that I felt pretty uncomfortable. I*
> *moved away from him and stayed close to my*
> *girlfriend that night, because I wasn't sure what*
> *he was trying to do. I'm just telling you this*
> *because at some of the parties you go to a friend*
> *of a friend may show up and try to intimidate*
> *you or pressure you to do sexual things you*
> *don't want to do. Slapping a girl or telling her*
> *he will spread lies about her are examples of*
> *force he might use. Even guys you know well might*
> *do that."*

Other related behaviors which could be included in such a story: guys lining the school hallway, calling out grades on girls' bodies; obscene phone calls; abusive jokes; pursuing someone relentlessly; girls patting a boy's crotch.

> *"One of the ways a sexual assault might happen is if you are at one of your friend's houses and her father tries to force you into sex. He might not have to tell you not to say anything because he knows you wouldn't want to hurt your friend's feelings."*

> *"My sister was really upset one day when we were teenagers. She had just come home from her friend's house. She wouldn't tell us what was the matter until days later. Finally she said she had been going swimming with her friend but forgot a towel. Her friend sent her into the house for one. Her friend's father, who had been mowing the lawn, followed her into the house and grabbed her from behind. She was able to resist and tell him 'no' and he backed off but she was still upset."*

> *"Here's a tough situation: say you are on a date with a guy for the second time, and you think you like him but you aren't sure you trust him. He suggests you go park and then drives to a deserted spot where you feel unsafe. He's a lot stronger than you and he has the car. It's hard to continue to resist if he insists on sex."*

Most sexual exploitation is based on verbal manipulation. Some people make others feel sorry for them or just somehow maneuver them into the spot where it seems that saying 'no' is really awful. "You would if you loved me" is pretty obvious, but "Why are you here if you don't want to have sex with me?" is tougher to respond to without sounding foolish. And most of us, especially teens, don't like to sound foolish.

> *"A friend of mine when I was a teenager had been going out with the same boy for a long time. She really wanted to keep him because he was good-looking and had a part time job and was going to be successful. But he told her if she didn't have sex with him, he wouldn't be her boyfriend anymore. She gave in, but she wasn't happy about it."*

Sometimes boys get together and egg each other on into planning an assault on a girl.

> *"When I was in college my boyfriend always stuck close to me because he didn't trust his fraternity brothers. Some of them would get 'drunk and crazy,' as he said, and gang up on a girl."*

Parents can offer some concrete help to teens. The suggestions in this chapter can help *start* communication about sexual assault. Once that happens, teens will think of lots of similar examples to talk about and learn from. Teens who have information and their parents' support and backing will be less likely to be trapped into an assault.

When You Were A Boy

by Larry Batson

When you are a boy of 12 or so, getting some size, older women stop looking directly at you when you walk by. The ones who know you, neighbors and relatives still speak. But strange women never seem to make eye contact with you any more.

If you notice at all — and you're not likely to at first — you put it down to the way women are. It may even please you, as evidence of your masculinity, for that is the way women behave around men. Nobody told you so. But you've watched it all your life.

It doesn't occur to you that these women are afraid of you. That you are old enough and big enough to begin to be a threat.

Your circle of female acquaintances and potential friends stops growing. Your neighbors, your classmates, your family — that's about it. When you get a job, the circle widens, but not greatly.

You are a threat, a physical threat, to all females. To the ones who know you, too, but they take chances, set conditions, and try to control them.

You don't think of it that way. You never really consider how it must be to live under the threat of physical domination.

Yet, man and boy, you know physical fear. There are school bullies, dark streets in strange neighborhoods, angry shouting drunks.

But you don't think of yourself as a fear-maker. Or do you?

There are always women. To impress, to bully a bit, to ignore. You do these things, or attempt them, thoughtlessly and automatically.

For in adolescence you begin to use a new language, a code of sexual signals that you have been learning by observation. For the rest of your life you will communicate with the few women you know almost exclusively in that primitive code. Not entirely, not always intentionally, but those signals tend to jam other frequencies.

Almost never will you be able to tell a woman precisely what you are thinking or feeling. There aren't that many signals in the male-female code. You can say to another man without words, "Be my friend." But you can't send that signal to a woman, not clearly.

So you will play your role and the women you meet will stick to theirs. Until they know you well, it's safer. And they can't really know you.

Beyond friendship the best offer a man can make a woman who attracts him is, "Be mine and I won't hurt you. I won't let anyone else hurt you either." Some deal, huh? But those words, embroidered a bit, are your marriage vows. If you are lucky in marriage and both you and your wife try hard, you may break out of that code before you die. You may actually learn to communicate as well with your wife as you do with half a dozen close male friends.

But you are a man and you play a role that shuts you off from half the people in the world. At best you have only a dim perception of how women feel.

Once in a great while they reach you. They tell you they want to "take back the night." They want to be able to walk in safety on public streets after dark. No man can hear such a request without feeling shame.

From The *Minneapolis Star and Tribune*. Reprinted with permission.

Chapter 4

"No Questions Asked" And Other Prevention Strategies

You can increase the likelihood that your teens will avoid sexual assault by providing good information, setting limits ahead of time, offering no-questions-asked bailouts, talking about group pressure and helping teens recognize behaviors which might be clues to mistreatment.

No-Questions-Asked Bailouts

Sexual assaults often happen in situations where the victim feels stuck: no way out; no way home; no place to run; or no one to help. To counter the powerlessness, parents can offer their teens the ''No-Questions-Asked Bailout.''

"The kids came home from school the other day with an agreement that the school has provided for parents and kids to sign about drinking and driving. The parents promise to drive their kids home without saying anything if the son or daughter promises to call for a ride if they are drunk or high and shouldn't be driving. I thought it was a great plan. The kids and their friends thought it was kind of corny, and wouldn't sign it. But we did agree that they would call if that was ever the situation, and I would come pick

*them up. Some of the kids said their parents had similar
plans, like when there is a party at their house, the
kids hand over their car keys to the parents. Their
parents only give them back after they have checked to
be sure the kids can drive."*

This plan might also work as a self-protective approach to
acquaintance rape. The situations in which teens are
victimized often involve being somewhere they're not
supposed to be: breaking a rule; going into someone's house
when no one else is home; being isolated at a party. It is a
good idea for parents to offer the no-questions-asked bailout.

*"If you are with a guy, at his house let's say, and
he refuses to drive you home until you go to bed with
him and you're not supposed to be seeing this guy in
the first place and you know I'm going to hit the roof,
try to get to a phone to call me anyway. I will come
get you, no questions asked. I promise not to embarass
you in front of him. If you promise to call, I promise
not to say a word for a day, and then we will sit down
and talk about it. It is more important that you have
a way to protect yourself in those kinds of situations
than it is to worry about having broken a rule."*

or

*"Call Aunt Paula and Uncle Jack. We have an agreement
that their kids can call me for help in an emergency
and you can call them. They'll take you to their house.
Then you can call me to let me know where you are and
that you are all right. The next day, when we've both
had time to think, you can come home and we'll talk."*

or

> *"Your sister Chris is three years older and she*
> *drives. Call her if you need help. She'll pick you*
> *up and won't tell us till you are ready to talk*
> *about it."*

Because teens have broken a family rule, disobeyed, or been in the wrong place at the wrong time, does not mean they deserve to be raped, although that is often the way they feel. It helps to distinguish between the consequences for breaking the rule,

> *"You are responsible for the decision to let your*
> *friends into this house when you've been told it's*
> *not okay."*

and the responsibility for the sexual assault.

> *"I know you never expected something like this to*
> *happen, and I know you didn't ask for it to happen.*
> *It was his choice to trick you and assault you. He is*
> *responsible for that."*

Dealing With Group Pressures

Helping teens understand that people behave differently in groups may help them avoid or identify a difficult situation. Parents may believe teens are less likely to be victimized if they go to parties or on group dates instead of on single dates. It's been a traditional safeguard to send kids on double dates so they are safer, but group events and parties have their own dangers because of pressures the group can bring.

Everyone has experienced times when standing up for a belief meant going against what "everybody else" seemed to think was okay. Being different is hard, especially when people ask, "What's the matter, are you chicken or something?" Going against the group means risking the loss of friendship. Members of the group may also fear, if someone doesn't go along with the group actions, that he or she is then free to betray the rest and get them in trouble. Because of their fear, they may seem to be physically threatening to a member of the group who isn't going along with it. It's difficult to do what is right when friends are pressuring for something else.

To understand group pressures, teens need to understand that group or gang psychology helps individuals avoid personal responsibility. In a group or gang people will behave in ways they would never behave individually. Everyone has heard of gang rapes, some occurring in front of others at beach parties, or in fraternity houses, or in cars. People in crowds feel anonymous. They somehow sense that they won't be held personally responsible for what is done — it's someone else's fault, somebody else started it. Some defend themselves by saying they were afraid not to go along with the group.

Both girls and guys need to be told about this influence on people. Girls are most likely to be victimized. Guys need to be aware so that they are not victimized either directly or by going along with something they are ashamed of later.

Teens will have difficulty believing that their peers could take part in any activity like this. The lesson to teach is not "Don't trust your friends," but rather, "Be aware that even people you trust can, under some circumstances, take advantage of the friendship."

One mother's strategy to help counter this pressure was to suggest to her teens that they take the lead in setting a new direction for the group.

She says, "Most of your friends are neat people. If you are uncomfortable with the situation, they probably are too."

In a group situation, everybody has more at stake than in a one-on-one situation. A guy may be worried about not getting as far as his friends, or that his friends will tease him about letting a girl talk him out of something. Parties can turn from friendly get-togethers to "makeout sessions" and become setups for sexual assault with only a few leading the way. Or sometimes parties are planned as traps for girls.

Teens need several strategies for avoiding victimization both before and during group situations. Here are some ideas:

Before:

• Maintain your choices by having your own car or transportation, or knowing you can call your parents or other family members.

• Pay attention to how your feelings change. A situation may seem all right at first, but then become uncomfortable.

• Be prepared for pressure if dating someone who has a reputation for "scoring."

• Decide what you'll do if she/he starts to pressure you for more sexual contact than you're ready for or when you aren't interested.

• Practicing assertive responses can make resisting group pressure easier.

• Practice making choices based on what you want. It is

easier to resist pressure if you know what you like and don't like, what you want and don't want. Extend this practice to recognizing when you don't like the way someone acts around you — even your boyfriend's or girlfriend's new buddy.

- Practice responses to being taken advantage of in little ways (Is it fair he always uses your notes? ... she borrows your clothes?). It may not seem worth the trouble to make a point of these little ways people take advantage of you, but it is easier to avoid being taken advantage of in larger ways if you've practiced on less important issues first.

- Make decisions about how you want to be treated, and practice sticking by them. If being treated well is one of the expectations you have for a relationship, you will be less likely to accept bad treatment which might lead into a sexual assault.

- Assertiveness is no guarantee that you won't find yourself in a difficult group situation, so be prepared to take action when you're confronted with a problem.

During:

- Walk and act confidently; look directly at people. If you don't look afraid, others may be less likely to pick on you.

- Just continue to do whatever you are doing and get through the situation.

- Appeal to a friend who is part of the group for help.

- Know your own feelings, so you can tell how much fear and discomfort is normal for you in parties and social gatherings and how much means it isn't an okay situation after all and it's time to leave. Your friends may laugh and you may be afraid you'll get into trouble at home, but your feelings may be telling you you would rather not be there.

- If there is physical violence toward anyone, leave without question.

- If desperate, be prepared to be outrageous: break a window, yell to call attention to the situation, ring the doorbell, turn the music way up or off.

One adult relates what happened to her as a teenager:

"One summer when I was in high school my girl friend and I were invited to a party. She and I were out shopping all day and didn't talk to our friends like we usually did before a party. Because we weren't sure who was going to be there, we weren't even sure we wanted to go. But each of us was leaving with our families on vacation the next week, so we decided we would see our friends one more time before going.

"When we got to the party, only guys were there. I wanted to leave right away, but my girl friend wanted to stay and see who might still be coming. Suddenly one of the guys shoved me down on the couch. I knew something awful was going on so I looked around for help. One of the guys sitting there was a good friend of mine. I looked up at him and said, 'What is going on here?' as emphatically as I could. He said, 'Come on, I'll get you out of here.' I found out later

that the same group of guys did rape a girl from another town the next weekend. I felt lucky I had gotten out, although I didn't understand how those guys could do such an awful thing.''

Talking About Limits

Parents sometimes hesitate to talk about family values and to set guidelines and limits on sexual behavior, although parents rarely hesitate to talk about and set limits on other behaviors. Since the move away from sexual repression, and the advent of more effective birth control, some parents have been reluctant to say ''no'' to sex. Others who have continued to say ''no'' find that ''no'' is not enough if teens do not have adequate information to help them make good decisions about sex.

Teenagers who have talked about sexual limits ahead of time are more able to avoid being exploited and/or pressured into exploiting another. They are much more likely to be able to figure out what to do when someone pressures for sex in the back seat of a car, or when alcohol appears, or when the group wants to do something hurtful to someone.

A lot of teenage sexual exploration is mutually exploitive. Neither partner understands the concept of consent. There is much evidence suggesting that both girls and boys have sexual intercourse for reasons other than the desire to do so, such as wanting to fit in with the crowd, to get affectionate touching, or to feel powerful and in control. They don't understand that sex should be related to caring and relationships.

"Every time I went out with a guy when I was a teen, it turned into a wrestling match in the back seat of the car.''

An acceptance of "giving in" to unwanted touching and a tolerance to being pressured seems to be learned. These are the attitudes that help create rape. To help overcome this influence, parents can talk to their children about sexual limits, family values and guidelines.

For instance, a parent's guidelines about acceptable and unacceptable dating behaviors might include: time expected home; unacceptable places to be because they are isolated and hard to get help from (such as "Lovers' Lane"); if they are going to park, park close to home; unacceptable behaviors (drinking, drugs, unchaperoned parties); a minimum age for the first date.

Talking about limits on sexual behavior would include: minimum age for sexual intercourse; what sexual behaviors are acceptable; unacceptable reasons for intercourse.

"It is not okay to have intercourse just because you feel like it. Your body may be able to conceive and bear children, but you're not ready to have a child."

"Being involved in a sexual relationship is very intense. If you are so absorbed in this, what else won't you be doing? You have lots of other things to be doing and learning about."

"Birth control does sometimes fail. Even though the risk of that is pretty low, the consequences are pretty high. It doesn't make any sense to risk something that could have such a destructive effect on your life, and on those who care about you."

"An early unpleasant sexual relationship can make it more difficult to have a satisfying one later in life."

"Some people think that once you have had sex it means you've made a commitment forever, as if you'll get married."

"If your date wants to do something you're not sure about, say you want time to think about it. You deserve to have time to decide for yourself."

"Don't ever use sex to hurt or gain power over another."

"I talked to my 15 year-old daughter because of my concern. I told her that friends and dates will sometimes try to take advantage of her by pressuring her for more sex than she is ready for. I felt a bit awkward, and I think she did too, but she listened. Next time we talk I'll try to make sure she understands that there may be times when she feels ready for more sexual contact but then isn't comfortable and wants to change her mind about continuing. I want her to know that it's okay to change her mind."

Although many adolescents are sexually active, most wait at least until they're 17 or 18. Half delay even longer. They need parental support for resisting pressures to have sex before they're ready. Pressures vary from simple peer influence to obvious force.

"Remember that girl at summer camp who had sex with a a boy and then he told everybody? After that everybody at school wanted to take her out. I want you to know that just because a girl or boy says yes once doesn't mean they have to keep saying yes."

"My 16 year old son came home from a party looking

troubled. I asked him what was wrong and his response was, 'Mom, tell me again why I shouldn't do it.' ''

"I'm not sure most of my reasons for wanting her to avoid adding sex to a relationship will be convincing, but I know I don't want her to be taken advantage of — she's too young to handle such hurt. I know I can't protect her from hurt, but I would like her to have more experience with relationships before she adds sex to one."

"My son needs and deserves more information about sex and dating than I got from my parents. I figure that part of my job is to provide a good example. I used to make comments about women's bodies and I gave that up. I don't want his mom, or his sister being treated like that. I hope my change will lessen his confusion about girls and sex and all that."

Some other ideas to help teens resist pressure:

- You don't have to have sex to get or keep a relationship.

- If he threatens you to try to get sex, he doesn't care very much about you.

- Sex should never be a test of love.

- You don't have to have sex, or even want sex, to be a man.

- Dares don't have to be taken.

Be specific. Teens will understand better and remember more.

> *"When I was a teenager anything past necking, which usually meant hugging and kissing, wasn't okay. Petting, which meant touching breasts or putting hands under clothes, just wasn't allowed. People thought that once you started that, it was pretty tough to stop. Now values are a lot more confused, but it's probably still true that petting is a new place to decide whether or not to continue or stop."*

> *"I remember boys who wanted to French kiss — which means tongue kissing — before I did. That really felt intrusive. When it is wanted, it usually increases the voltage in a relationship."*

Teens need to hear parents say that pushing, manipulating, pressuring, exploiting, or abusing another person is not acceptable.

Pushing "Let's leave this party and learn about each other. All the other girls do it."

Manipulating "You can't tease me and leave me."

"I want to make you feel like a woman."

"If I can't have you, there is no reason to live."

Pressuring	"You're still a virgin! What are you, frigid?"
	"It will help our relationship grow."
	"I'll find someone else who will."
Exploiting	"Here, have another beer. You'll feel friendlier."
	"You're my girl friend and you owe it to me."
Abusing	"You should be grateful."
	"You're so ugly nobody else would want you."

It is from listening to and testing family values that teens form their own. Teens who can set sexual limits are much less likely to be taken advantage of.

Avoiding Potential Offenders

Parents often try to monitor their children's dates and friends. With teens, that screening can create more trouble than it avoids. Teens are very loyal to their friends and any negative statements about them by parents just leads them to defend their friends more intensely.

Some parents of girls simply look upon all boys as exploiters. There is a cartoon in which the father opens the front door and greets his daughter's date with "Hello, rapist."

Parents in the past have tended to rely on manners as an indication of how a young man will treat their daughter, or on "morals" as an indicator about whether or not a girl will "get their boys into trouble." However all rape crisis workers have heard victims say, "My parents thought he was so nice because he was so polite."

Some studies of teen rapists find that they come from good families, and are involved in extracurricular activities, such as sports and church groups. The best course of action considering this is to prepare teens to respect their own judgement and suspicions and let them know they must decide about somone.

The following are signals a parent can give a teen as clues to begin a self-protective response. They are clues that someone may be willing to take advantage of another or be assaultive. These actions may or may not mean that a sexual assault is next. But they may be the only warning a teen gets.

"Someone who...
　...doesn't care for your feelings
　...ignores what you say
　...talks over you, as though you're not there
　...pretends not to hear you
　...never looks at you
　...teases you about something she knows you're
　　　really sensitive about
　...acts more friendly when you're alone than when
　　　his friends are around
　...does what she wants regardless of what you want
　...is hostile when you don't go along with him
　...sulks when you don't do what she wanted to do
　...shows or uses violence in other situations to
　　　get his way...

...may not care enough about you to listen when you say
'no'.''

What is important is whether the person cares about
others or does what he or she wants regardless of who is hurt
or what the rules are.

Some teens express the idea that good looking guys
wouldn't have to rape. The opposite sometimes turns out to
be true. Sometimes the good looking or successful guys
assume they have the "right" to sex, and will stop at nothing
to get it. Parents can point out the problem by saying,

> *"Sometimes people who are really popular — maybe*
> *stars at school   or much older, think they have rights*
> *to tell you what to do. Is there anyone at your school*
> *who acts like that?"*

Other studies have found links between participating in
delinquent activities and committing sexual assaults. Loyalty
to a delinquent peer group, low attachment to school or
family, and a high number of family crises were associated
with involvement in delinquent activities. However, these
associations were not absolute. Some teen boys without these
characteristics did commit sexual assault and a number of
boys with these characteristics did not commit a sexual
assault. It is not that easy to predict who will be an offender.

Using this information, parents could talk about potential
danger signs, before their teens are dating or running around
with anyone. Parents could say something such as,

> *"You know, kids who don't care about their family or*
> *school are more likely to mistreat the people they*
> *date or run around with."*

or

> *"People who ignore rules about drugs or school or alcohol sometimes think they don't have to obey the rules about how to treat other people. Sometimes they are aggressive just because they know they can get away with it."*

Personal Space

It is helpful if teens know that intrusions into their personal space are often the first steps in a sexual assault. Even when warning feelings alert us that someone is trespassing on our personal space, they are easy to ignore. No one wants to believe that friends would be exploitive, and usually people don't mean any harm. But sometimes they are the beginning of breaking down resistance to further invasion.

Examples of these intrusions are when someone:
...stands or sits too close
...is always touching
...touches your breast "by accident"
...stares even after you break eye contact
...stares at the sexual parts of your body.

Although it is difficult to know just when to take these signals seriously, they may be important warning signals.

Discussion Starters

"Dear Abby" game

While teens feel that nothing bad will happen to them, they do see that others sometimes have problems. To get teens to consider situations ahead of time, parents could ask their teens to answer a typical advice column letter about sexuality and/or sexual abuse:

> *"This kid I know has a babysitting job with a family in the neighborhood. She babysits a lot after school for the mother, but sometimes she is asked to sit in the evening too. She doesn't like the father because for years he has stared at her. What can she do?"*

Question Box

In a busy household a "question box" could be used so questions don't get forgotten just because there is no one around to answer them when they are thought of. It will be used more if adults ask questions they have about teen behavior and activities.

Teen "What if...?" game

What if —

> *"You and your boy friend had planned to go to a movie, but when he comes to pick you up, he announces you're going to a party. You know there are no parents home, because everyone was talking about the party at school. You told your boy friend you didn't want to go to it, but now he is pressuring you."*

"You're home alone and one of your dad's friends comes by to borrow something. You can smell the alcohol on his breath and he is asking to come in, even though you've told him your dad isn't home."

"You're staying overnight at your girlfriend's and her parents leave. The next thing you know, her older brother has brought some of his friends home and you feel uncomfortable."

"You're with a group of guys who begin planning a big beer party and then start talking about which girl they can trick into coming to the party."

Chapter 5

Self-Esteem: A Tool For Protection

If teens feel they deserve to be treated well, they will recognize and resist being treated badly.

Teens who have a realistic sense of their own worth — "I know that some kids like me because I have at least some good friends." "I'm a safe driver and don't get traffic tickets." "I feel good about being able to stand up for myself when someone is trying to push me around." — are in a better position to recognize and resist pressures of all kinds. They will be able to recognize and resist sexual exploitation or the pressures that may be leading up to an assault. Teens who feel confident of their own judgement will be less susceptible to manipulation by others who say such things as, "What's the matter, chicken?" or "I won't like you any more if you don't do this."

Parents may feel handicapped in offering help for a teen's self-esteem since teens don't seem to care much for their parents' opinion about so many things. But despite appearances, teens do want and need parental approval, support, and praise.

Here are three strategies parents can use to help build self-esteem:

- Notice and express appreciation of specific instances of competence. Teenagers need and want to be seen as competent.

  "I'm glad you're taking that speech class. I know you're scared sometimes, but knowing how to talk in public is really important. Lots of people never get over their fears, so being good at it gives you an edge over other folks."

  "I really appreciate how you take charge of making dinner when you know I'm going to be late getting home at night."

- Show respect for the teen's opinions and judgement.

  "We need to decide how to spend our summer vacation time and money. Do you have any ideas; anything you think we should or shouldn't do? I would like us to spend some of that time together."

- Provide activities outside the family which contribute to the teen's sense of accomplishment and achievement.

  "My daughter has shown an ability to see spatial relationships from the time she was three. So even though it takes extra time and energy, we've been providing art lessons with a teacher who really encourages her students' unique talents."

  "I'm really glad girls have more sports activities. Our oldest does well in soccer and gets many compliments because she runs well. She will have many opportunities to use her abilities as she gets older."

Talking

The way parents talk to and act toward their children indicates what they think of them and how they are expected to act. Although they may not always act like it, teens need to hear messages such as, "I'm glad you're you, I'm glad you're here, and I'm glad you're part of the family." They need some other messages specific to their stage in life:

- You can be a grownup and still need help and support and affection from other people.
- Sometimes you need to ask others to give you what you need.
- You are a knowledgeable, skillful and strong young person.
- You have shown responsibility in many ways. I've enjoyed watching you become responsible.
- I trust you to use good judgement.
- You have shown good sense to decide what rules to make your own.
- It is not up to you to make everybody like you.
- You never need to accept poor treatment from someone else.
- You can trust your feelings to help you know.
- You can do it your way.
- It's okay to disagree.
- You don't have to suffer, or be sick or miserable, to get what you need.
- I'm glad you're here, and I'm glad to see you are learning to do things your own way.
- You can be independent and grownup and still have needs for family and friends.
- I see you are growing into an attractive young person.
- You deserve to be treated well, with respect and caring.

Within The Family

Many families start when children are very young to allow them to make decisions about those things they are capable of deciding. The two year old gets to decide which pants he is going to wear, the five year old what she is going to eat for lunch, the ten year old whether she is going to turn out for soccer or be on a swim team, and a junior high schooler what electives to take.

Teens with no practice in decision making and little self-esteem tend to just go along with things until it is too late or too difficult to get out. Parents can give their teens as much practice at decision making as possible. When teens are accustomed to having decisions made for them, they are unlikely to be able to object when the decisions others make place them in danger.

As teens get older, they push for more and more decision making power. The challenge of parenting is to give them as much as they are ready for. This doesn't mean as many decisions as they can make without *making* mistakes, but rather as many as they can make and be able to *survive* the mistakes.

> *"In our family we have always worked with the kids to help them figure out what they liked and didn't like. We ask them questions like, 'What do you like about that, the color, or the sound?' and we have them describe what they liked so they learn how they are making their judgements. Whenever we can, we ask their opinions about household decisions. Their answers are sometimes not ones we can use — like the time they wanted to paint the walls red — but we ask."*

Other ways to indicate respect and caring in the family
are with touch and expressions of positive regard. Touch is
discussed in Chapter 7.

Some other ways of showing respect and caring:

Active listening is a tool for improving communication. Listen
for the emotional content of a statement and reflect that tone
in the return comment.

> Teen: *"My 3rd period teacher has all the attractive
> girls sit in the front row so he can look down their
> shirts."*
> Parent: *"That must be pretty upsetting."*
> Teen: *"It makes me really mad. I'm thinking about just
> yelling out in the middle of class what he is doing."*
> Parent: *"You want him to stop. Do you think that will
> do it?"*
> Teen: *"I'm not sure."*
> Parent: *"Do you want some help figuring out your
> alternatives?"*
> (This teen decided to say quietly to her teacher, "I know
> what you're doing and if you don't stop I'm going to tell.")

Specific praise is welcome when it is specific enough so the
child does not feel the parent is passing judgement. With
teens it is helpful if the praise is screened to see whether it
would be welcomed by another adult. If not it may be better to
pass.

"Your room looks nice today," may be a little too obvious
when there has been a war over the state of the room. "I
really appreciate the cleanup job on the car," is praise anyone
would be glad to hear.

Smiles and eye contact may be difficult to maintain when teens seem to withdraw and avoid our eyes. Teens may be uncomfortable with prolonged eye contact, but they don't mind that quick acknowledgement of their presence.

Letting kids in on parent's moods can help kids sort out what is their responsibility from what else is going on. If a parent growls at a kid, even an older teen is likely to feel in the wrong. It is better to say, "I'm not mad at you, but I had a miserable day and I am not in the mood to be sociable (or talk about the car) right now."

Outside The Family

Parents can participate with their children in religious, ethnic, sports, or other community activities. Although parents don't always realize it, these activities convey community standards and provide opportunity for discussion of those values.

This also gives parents an opportunity to see other teens and their parents and know how other families deal with growing up issues. That way, teens realize their parents know what community standards are and when "everybody else" *is* doing it and when they aren't. That sometimes makes it easier to stick to a decision.

> *"My sixth grader had been nagging at me to let her wear nylons for more than a year. Even though I knew that some of the girls had been wearing them since the fourth grade, I had decided there was plenty of time for nylons after elementary school. At the fall concert, the woman next to me commented on the half of the girls still wearing tights and knee highs. We exchanged support of each others' stand, saying kids*

*are growing up too early and need to be kids, not
adults. Without seeing the other kids and knowing
other parents were holding out, I would be more
susceptible to my daughter's pressure."*

Of course sometimes parents will find themselves saying,
"I know that is different from what others are doing, but that
is how we are going to do it." Their credibility is even
stronger for knowing it is different from the norm.

Research findings suggest that girls involved with their
families in church activities, regardless of the church's
teachings about sexuality, delay beginning sexual intercourse
longer than girls who were not involved in such activities with
their families. This suggests that these girls were more sure
of their family values, and could resist pressure to go against
them because of the opportunity for discussion with their
parents.

Other shared activities may function in a similar
mannner. Sports can teach teamwork and cooperation.
Granges, some 4-H and other youth groups teach community
cooperation, sportsmanship, self-discipline and specific
achievement, respect and thoughtfulness for others. Parents
who monitor and are involved in community activities can
notice and talk to their teens about values with which they
disagree, and state their agreement with those which teach
respect and caring.

*"One of the soccer teams my daughter's team plays
is really rough and the parents on that side do a
lot of nasty yelling at the referee. On the way home
from the game we talked about winning, and teamwork
and competition and fairness. I want her to learn
to exert and push herself and learn about her own*

limits, but not get into the 'kill 'em' and win at all costs.''

''At a school concert the other night, the students sang a song with the words 'Freedom is just a state of mind.' My husband and I think that there are real barriers to freedom for minority groups, women, and others in this country. The song reminded me that the belief that anyone in this country can be anything he or she wants to be is taught in the schools. I will need to explain my belief to the contrary.''

These activities also provide non-dating social interaction between boys and girls, allowing them to know each other as people. Teens who know the other sex as people are less vulnerable to exploitation as victim or victimizer.

''My daughter seems to be able to be friends with boys in her classes because she talks about and is interested in skiing, soccer and animals. So far she is resisting the pressure to be interested in boys just because they are boys.''

Another advantage of these activities is that parents can stress accomplishment of a variety of talents and skills. The teen who has specific accomplishments is in a better position to say, 'no' to those activities which are solely for the purpose of belonging.

Self-Esteem And The Assault Victim

All teens need to hear that their parents believe they are capable, trustworthy persons. But teenagers who have been

sexually assaulted especially need help increasing their
feelings of self-worth. This is particularly important because
teens who've been assaulted once seem to be vulnerable to
being victimized again.

Victims of assault or exploitation may feel diminished,
fragile, angry, dependent or isolated and especially need
loving words of support from the adults in their lives. Parents
need to model and say, "You can trust people. You can decide
who to trust. And you can be independent and make your own
decisions without giving in to others. We trust you to do
that."

Even victims of earlier child sexual abuse who appear to
have healed need parental rediscussions of the abuse as they
enter puberty at ages 10 - 14. "We know that you're okay and
that we talked about it back then, but sometimes when young
teens are trying to make decisions about sex, love, or
relationships, they may have questions again about how you
can know who to trust and when. We just want you to know
that's okay."

                    *   *   *

"It is not up to you to make everybody like you." Adolescents
need to feel part of a peer group, or have a sense of
belonging. They frequently succumb to pressure or force from
friends to break family rules. Parents can add: "You don't
have to use drugs and alchohol and have sex as a proof of
friendship or love; you can say no."

*"You never need to accept poor treatment from someone
else."* Parents can help their child recover from feelings of
being damaged and undeserving of good relationships. "You
deserve good relationships. You deserve love and affection.

Though someone treated you badly, you are still whole; nothing has been taken from you."

Parents can explain that there is the possibility for poor treatment in every part of our lives: home, school, work and social or romantic relationships. But whatever the source or place, none are deserved or right. Every young person deserves to be treated well.

"You are a competent and powerful young person." "You are able to make decisions and act on them. You can be in charge of what happens to you, and how you feel about it."

Many assault victims feel unable to say no. They may feel they have no control over their lives. Parents can help by encouraging safe opportunities where the young person can succeed, such as going shopping alone, or choosing their own clothing. "Yes, something terrible happened to you. That doesn't mean that you are terrible."

"You have the good sense to decide what rules to make on your own." Abuse victims may distrust their ability to make decisions and protect themselves against future abuse. Teens need parental support in relearning to trust their "gut feelings" about people and situations. They will need specific suggestions for avoiding or getting out of situations that feel risky.

"You don't have to suffer to get what you need." Some abuse victims don't feel loved unless they are abused. Being exploited or abused should never be expected as a proof of love. The abuse may cause some abuse victims to see themselves as criminal or unworthy. Parents can say, "Healthy relationships don't require pain and suffering."

"You can do it your way. You can disagree." Many victims
are taught not to question the abuser's authority or power and
become compliant. Parents can help children learn to value
their own opinions and feelings and how to assert themselves
when someone is pressuring for sex. Discussions about family
rules are good opportunities for young people to challenge
and contribute to the expectations that govern their lives.

"You don't have to be sexual to meet your needs." Some
victims will need help to regain their sense of control over
their own sexuality, to learn or relearn that they can choose if,
when, and with whom they will be sexual. They may feel that
their need to say no has been stolen. Parents can make it clear
that "no" is always theirs to say.

Parents can help their teens learn how to ask for and give
affection, and how to say no to unwanted touch. They can
discuss the differences between nurturing, affectionate, and
sexual touch. And they can talk about how everyone needs a
number of affectionate, intimate, non-sexual relationships
with peers, relatives, neighbors, and friends at work or at
school.

With this help, assaulted teens will be better able to
avoid revictimization.

Chapter 6

Messages And Myths: The Influence Of The Media

The media powerfully influence teenagers. Kids are getting messages about themselves and their sexuality not only from peers, school, church, and parents, but also from television, movies, books, music, record album covers, posters, and magazines. Daily they hear a variety of messages:

- Buy these jeans — you'll be gorgeous and popular
- This makeup will make you beautiful
- When you are good looking everyone will love you
- If you are macho and handsome, women will want you
- Drink beer, it's fun
- Real men are tough
- Women love being roughed up once in a while.

The list could go on — and most teenagers could add to it. While they recognize some of the media hype and fantasy for what it is, the media is a problem because of the power and content of its messages. It affects us whether or not we realize it.

What are teens really learning? Media messages can increase a teenager's confusion about sexuality: Am I okay?

(Even though I'm not: seductive, macho, white, pretty, handsome, rich...?)

> *Discussion Starter*: List with your kids the
> subtle (and not so subtle) messages from TV ads,
> like "the human body is smelly and unclean," and
> "ring around the collar is a social disaster."

There has been a lot of discussion about television and its effect on children. Parents have been encouraged to watch TV with kids, so that parents can point out the media messages and help their kids learn to question what they are seeing rather than just taking it all in.

It is tempting to hope that our kids are getting an adequate sex education from all that they read and see. Today's teens have been exposed to more sexually explicit information than any previous generation. Within one generation, prime time TV has moved from married couples who could not be seen together in bed, to nudity, to couples acting as if engaged in intercourse, to rape, live birth, and sexually explicit humor. Teenagers are under a lot of pressure to be "sexy," to know about sex, and to have sex. But the media is generally not a sex educator to trust. It teaches sexual values that may not be in agreement with each family's own values.

TELEVISION AND SEXUAL VALUES

Do the programs you and your children watch show:

WOMEN:

- Primarily as self-sacrificing, home-bound wives and mothers
- Working at a career at the expense of happiness
- As adventurous, succesful risk-takers
- In roles of power and responsibilty
- Acting seductively in enticing costumes.

MEN:

- Primarily as wage-earners
- As nurturing and socially aware
- Who must repeatedly prove their physical and sexual prowess.

RELATIONSHIPS:

- Showing men and women interacting as equals
- Frequently characterized by conflict and sexual violence
- In which non-sexual affection is shown
- Where family life is portrayed as mainly the concern of women
- Where human sexuality is characterized as dirty or illicit
- Where men overpower the women.

(Adapted from a classroom exercise by Barbara McGuire, Educator, Planned Parenthood, Seattle-King County, Washington. Used by permission.)

One of the media's worst aspects is its frequent linking of sex and violence. There are ads and rock videos which feature women who are tied down, physically threatened, being hit. There are T.V. shows in which characters fall in love with those who raped them. On other T.V. shows, the sexy male and female detective team may shoot the ''bad guy,'' and congratulate each other with a long kiss, standing over the body — gun still in hand. The media knows the two things that sell: sex and violence. What are kids learning? That violence is sexy? That sex usually involves violence?

> Parents can raise their children's ability to pick out media messages by going through a magazine and discussing what they see in the ads.

Many messages about sex and violence are not subtle at all. In pornography, abusive, degrading, dominating sexual material is aimed at selling a product or to entertain. It used to be rare for teens to have easy access to pornography — at the very least, they had to leave their home. Now any home with cable TV can subscribe to soft core pornography channels. Many families have video machines and can rent videos on any subject. Pornographic magazines are available at the corner drug store and grocery. Many ads in popular magazines use a combination of sex, romance, and violence to sell their products. According to the film *Not A Love Story,* produced by the National Film Board of Canada, there are four times as many pornographic bookstores in the U.S. as there are McDonald's restaurants.

*"Some junior high school boys in our neighborhood
had taken one of their father's soft core porn
magazines. They made a big deal of it — hiding
it from my two daughters. They were laughing and
giggling about the pictures. The boys, obviously,
weren't sure what to think. My daughters came home
and asked me if people really did that. I said 'yes'
and they said, 'Oh, GROSS!!' I let that drop, but
said that it was too bad the boys' only source of
information was the magazine. When sexual
intercourse really doesn't make much sense, how
much more confusing are the other variations on
human sexuality, especially as conveyed in 'men's'
magazines."*

What Can Parents Do?

Teens aren't getting the information they need.
Numerous studies find that though teenagers appear to be
more sophisticated than their parents were as kids, they have
little accurate information about positive, healthy sexuality.
The media feeds their confusion.

One approach parents use is to forbid sexually explicit
material altogether (no *Hustler*, dirty books or raunchy music
in the house; no going to X-rated films; no watching the adult
cable channels, etc.).

One problem with that approach can be that teens may
interpret the adult message as, "It's dirty because it's sex.
It's bad stuff, but I can't tell you why," when the real
message is, "It's forbidden because it's violent, it's powerful,
and it's going to influence how you are 'turned on' sexually."

Many parents fear this approach for its "forbidden fruit"
effect. Though we may not worry about setting other limits on

our children's sexual lives (discouraging public masturbation by young children), we wonder if forbidden things will become more desirable. Not necessarily:

> *"I was prepared for the worst when I decided to eliminate sugar from the house. I thought it would make the kids really go for it at other people's houses, or at school. But it had the opposite effect. They really understand now that they just feel better without it and they turn it down when it's offered at their friends'."*

A second approach is to accept, or at least tolerate, soft core pornography (*Playboy* pinups on the wall, for example). The hope is that being open and positive about a child's sexual expressions will encourage open communication. This may work, but it also carries the message that it's okay to make women into sex objects. It doesn't help kids make the connection we want them to make between sex and loving. *Playboy* pin-ups also...

...imply that the idealized, glamorized body is a good one, the one all girls should have,

...set up expectations for boys that they will have sex with a fantasy figure of perfection few teen boys will ever know, let alone have sex with,

...make both boys and girls feel impotent, as if they are less than they "should" be.

Parents make the difference between kids who are confused by the mixed messages and kids who are able to sort out the garbage. The media has the greatest influence where the teenage viewer is least informed. Teens with no other source of information about attractiveness, sex, and rape will depend on the media more than teens with other resources.

To lessen the impact, parents can provide their kids with accurate information. While we can't change the whole world tomorrow, nor entirely remove the media's influence, we can provide positive, healthy alternative messages.

One way to begin communication is to find out what teenagers already know. A Minneapolis survey asked teens to define pornography. Most said it was movies, books, photos, or magazines with sex or nudity. Teenagers, like most people, don't usually have much notion of what pornography is. Only a few said that it is "exploiting someone," "children posing for nude pictures," "flaunting the human body," "portraying sex in a vulgar way," or "selling sex." Most did not understand that pornography always mixes violence, exploitation, abuse or degradation with sex. What teens know and don't know is always a surprise. Asking is the best way to start.

TAKE BACK THE NIGHT
Women on Pornography
Edited by Laura Lederer
New York: William Morrow and Company, Inc., 1980

A good book if more information is needed to understand pornography or make decisions about it. Defines and describes pornography: who is hurt, who benefits, research findings, pornography and the First Amendment, and action strategies. Contributors include Marge Piercy, Susan Griffin, Robin Morgan, and Susan Brownmiller.

When starting a discussion about something as difficult as pornography, it's easier to start with a definition. Not all sexually explicit material is pornographic.

• *Pornography* is sexually explicit material which
portrays abuse, violence, and degradation for the
purpose of arousal and entertainment.
• *Erotica* describes sexual materials which may or
may not be sexually explicit and are used for the
purpose of arousal and entertainment. Erotica does
not include violence, abuse, or degradation of a person.
• *Sexuality education materials* are sexually
explicit materials used for the purpose of education or
therapy which do not include violence, abuse, or
degradation.

(Definitions from *Sexual Violence: The Unmentionable
Sin*, by Marie Marshall Fortune. New York: Pilgrim
Press, 1983.)

People disagree about whether pornography is harmful
and encourages violence, or is educational and a form of
human sexual expression. Some people argue that it helps
men work out their aggression in a safe way. Some believe
that sexual offenses, like rape, would decrease if more men
had access to pornography and that it is a valid way to learn
about sex without the risks of trying it.

However, recent research indicates that the more people
watch images of violence, the more likely they are to employ
violence. As more violence is seen, viewers become
increasingly numb to it, and more is needed to cause a
reaction. One study found that college age men who viewed
porn that blended sex and violence tended to be more aroused

by the idea of rape, and less sympathetic to the victims, than men who hadn't seen pornography. The researchers state that "one exposure to violence in pornography can significantly influence erotic reactions to the portrayal of rape." When asked if they felt they would commit a rape if they were sure they wouldn't be caught, 51 per cent of those college age men responded they would.

Why this confusion about the role of pornography? Marie Fortune, in *Sexual Violence*, outlines two common views of pornography:

CONSERVATIVE
sex = bad
pornography = sex
therefore: pornography = bad

LIBERAL
sex = good
pornography = sex
therefore: pornography = good

The problem here is that *sex is not equal to pornography.*

What Can I Say?

Our goals should be to help our kids understand the difference between pornography (abusive sex) and erotica (consensual, equal sex). When they are exposed to images of sexual violence in pornography, on record album covers, in music, etc., we want them to be able to choose. They should be able to say, "This is not okay because...." "This is gross because...."

Carol: *What are we going to give grandpa for his birthday
   this year?*

Leon: *I want to give him a year's subscription to*
   Playboy. *I think he'd get a kick out of it.*

Carol: *If you want to give him that from you...OK, but
   please don't put my name on the card. I don't want to
   be involved in giving that sort of thing for a gift.*

Leon: *Why? I think he'd really enjoy it.*

Carol: *I don't like how women are treated there —
   they're only beautiful, only women with gorgeous
   bodies — and sex seems like something people do
   between tennis and a fancy dinner out — just
   another activity for the young and the beautiful.
   I don't want to be seen as giving that as a gift.
   I'm not going to stop you, or start a fight about
   it... but I'll find something else for a gift from
   the kids and me.*

Leon: *Well, I hadn't thought about* Playboy *that way...
   I don't think I agree that it's all that bad, but
   I'd rather give something from all of us, so what
   else can we give, what does he need, what would he
   like?*

Carol: *I really appreciate your going along with me on
   this. What about taking him out to dinner, or making
   dinner here for grandpa and his girlfriend?*

   Part of the problem in helping them to reach this level of
understanding is that they need a positive picture of sexuality

from elsewhere if they are indeed to make a choice. The media, unfortunately, don't offer much in that light, but parents can. Parents can actively search out the positive in magazines or books or on TV, and model affectionate, loving behavior such as hugs and morning rituals for nurturing each other.

> *"I liked that movie. It showed guys and girls caring for each other as friends."*

> *"These are nice photos. They show men and women as ordinary, but still okay, attractive people."*

> *"I recently found my 13 year old daughter at home listening to some records that had the most awful album covers. Something involving women in chains, nearly nude, being hurt, bleeding and of course loving it. I told my daughter that I couldn't abide that kind of message about women in my house and to dispose of it. She thought I was going off the deep end. She said she knew the cover was crummy but that I wasn't being fair. I thought she got rid of it, but later I found it hidden. I realize, now, I was asking her to do better than I do. Plenty of my magazines have objectionable ads, and I don't cancel my subscription."*

> *"I found I was making some rules about TV my kids refused to keep. I still felt strongly, but I tried another tack. Now sometimes when they are home dancing in front of the videos or the TV, I join them. We talk about the stuff on the video. How people think it's cool to treat girls like sex objects, and how boys act like all they want is*

*sex. Although it's pretty awful stuff, we've been
able to see how ridiculous it is and laugh at it.''*

The most effective approach may be to tell your kids
about what you think. For example:

*''I don't like that magazine. I think the overall
message is for men to conquer women.''*

*''I don't like the way the women in that magazine
are all in silly poses for men to stare at them
like they are pieces of meat.''*

*''I don't think ads should use children in sexual
poses to sell jeans. It's not right to make people
think that children are available to them sexually.''*

These statements are also useful discussion starters,
especially if used with questions: ''Do you think that's really
right?'' ''Does it seem that way to you?'', or ''Am I seeing
this the same way you are?''

Mom: *I was reading in the paper this morning that
       'Porky's' was a multimillion dollar hit.
       You saw that movie, didn't you?*

Son: *Yeah, I went last summer with Jo, remember?*

Mom: *What did you think of it?*

Son: *It was okay.*

Mom: *The paper also said that it was a film
       which showed girls as sex objects for*

*guys to stare at through holes in the
locker room walls. That it kind of treated
girls like they were in two categories: fat
ugly ones to be real cruel to, or the
gorgeous sex objects. It said the girls
didn't have names, or feelings, or
friendships like the boys did.*

Son: *It's just a movie, Mom! Why do you take it
so seriously?*

Mom: *Because media messages are very powerful.
They can influence how you feel about
girls and about sex. You know, a lot of
people think it's okay to act that way?*

Son: *Not me, I'm not affected by that stuff.*

Mom: *How do you know you're not affected?
How did Jo feel about it? Was she
uncomfortable?*

Even if parents are not sure what to think about some of
these issues, you can still talk about them. Nobody has all the
answers. The key is to keep the dialogue open.

"Our girls found a Playboy *on our bookshelves
that a visiting relative had left. I suggested they
bring it to family meeting so we could talk about it.
They had a lot of questions, some of which I couldn't
really answer, like 'Why are there only women? Don't
they feel silly posing like that? Is this pornography?
What's wrong with it?' Now they want to see a*
Playgirl *to see if the men are posed in the same*

way. I did end up having a good talk about it with them. I reassured them that their sense of exposure was valid — that it wasn't the nudity, it was the way they were posed. I told them I was bothered, too, and that I thought it was sad. I told them that no women really look that way — that the photos are touched up, and that the women got paid for posing but that it was a hard way to earn money."

Parents can turn the media into an active tool for learning. They can encourage their children to think about what they see and hear. It is often easier to get a discussion going about a TV or movie character's problems and feelings than it is to discuss your teenager's own problems or feelings.

Chapter 7

Just Friends:
Overcoming Sex Role Expectations

Boys and girls are raised to think so differently about themselves, sex, affection, and force that they have little understanding of each other.

> *"I guess it's hard to believe a girl would really mind that much, because the guy's never even imagined a negative sexual experience. He can't quite relate to the significance of coercion. After all sex is fun, right?"* (From "Date Rape, a Campus Epidemic," by Karen Barrett. *Ms.* Magazine, September, 1982.)

Sex role differences, such as girls trained to resist, and boys to push, are considered by some professionals to be a setup for acquaintance rape. Although it was hoped that recent societal changes would make it easier for girls to refuse sexual activity when they didn't want it and accept when they did, there is still much confusion about male/female roles.

> *"My boy is getting telephone calls all the time and he doesn't know how to handle it. My husband is very traditional and he keeps calling the girls whores. That makes my son mad. It's a mess at our house."*

*"It seems to me that all that sexual equality has
done is leave girls unprotected. At least in our day,
'good girls' didn't get pressured. The boys knew where
they stood and left them alone."*

*"My son is being pressured to be sexually active by
his girlfriend and his friends. He says he isn't
ready yet. I'm proud of his independence and want to
help him stick to his decision as long as he would
like, but he is getting tired of all the name
calling and harassment."*

Parents can lessen the effects of sex role stereotypes by
providing information about sex roles, encouraging
friendships with teens of both sexes, and discussing the
confusion which arises from the different ways boys and girls
see the world.

To start, parents need to know how sex role stereotypes
may affect their children. Even when parents want to raise
their children without restrictions based on gender, society —
in the form of media, relatives, school, coaches and other
parents — imposes expectations. Uncertain about what to say
to teens about dating and relationships, many parents are
reduced to saying either, "Watch out for those boys. They are
all after the same thing," or "Watch out for those girls. They
are only after your money," or "Don't get caught, or trapped
by some young thing." These warnings, though, have not
been adequate protection as the statistics on acquaintance
rape and teen pregnancies show. And they don't help teens
create the cooperative and friendly relationships parents
would like for them.

Here are some of the most common sex role stereotypes,
and some strategies for getting beyond them.

1. *Sex role stereotypes train girls to resist — that is to say "no" to sex — and boys to push for a "yes."*

Strategies

Teach teens to talk to each other. Teach girls to say what they mean, and teach boys to listen to the answer. Girls and boys both need *second* lines such as, "I know that some girls just say no because they think they should. Is that what you're doing?" Girls can learn practiced responses to standard lines, "Yes, I like you, but I like myself well enough to do what I want to do." or "I would rather do something else." "I like (love) you very much but I am just not ready to have sex with anyone. When I am ready, I'll say so."

Refusing sex may result in losing a boy or girl friend. Parents can acknowledge that and suggest that one of the signs of caring is a willingness to consider the other's needs, especially about something as important as sex.

Boys who don't push may find they are put down for that. Parents can talk about the difference between reasonable persistence and pushiness.

"After the fourth time it is pushiness, not persistence."

"If she asks to go home, you've been pushy."

"Checking out the reasons for a 'no' is okay. Telling a girl you'll stop dating her if she doesn't have sex with you isn't."

This distinction between force and reasonable persistence is lost on acquaintance rapists. They frequently phone those they have victimized, asking for another date, not realizing the extent of discomfort the assault has caused the victim.

2. *Sex role stereotypes make it difficult for boys to receive and give nurturing and affectionate touch without sexual overtones.*
(There is some evidence this is lessening in teens and pre-teens of the eighties.)

Strategies

Model and talk about different kinds of touch within the family. Teach boys and girls to ask for and give hugs or affectionate touch. Emphasize the importance of friendships and commitments to friends. Talk about how touching happens between friends of the same sex.

"Girls curl each others' hair, or try on makeup, each others' clothes. How about your friends? What do they do?"

"Boys pat each other on the back or push each other around, beat on each other. What can a girl and boy who are friends do?" (Some answers: pat each other on the back, neck rubs, foot massages, push each other around gently, take walks together, and talk.)

Parents can talk about how different touch is within a romantic context, and how ambiguous touch becomes if it seems a friendship is changing.

3. *Sex role steretoypes make it more difficult for girls to protect themselves.*

If girls are supposed to be nice, passive and submissive, it will be difficult for them to suddenly become aggressive in order to protect themselves. Girls often feel they have some kind of obligation to boys who may be attracted to them. They feel they should be nice, even if they don't like the guy or the way he treats them.

Strategies

It is not necessary to teach girls to be nicer than boys. Parents can make distinctions between being polite or considerate and always being nice. Rehearse specific responses, both physical and verbal, to trouble situations. For example girls can step back and straighten up if someone asks them an "iffy" question. They can speak loudly in response to someone getting too close. They can put out a hand for a handshake instead of submitting to an unwanted kiss or hug.

Practice firm, but not rude, responses to approaches. If the response is too harsh, girls may be afraid of hurting the guy's feelings, or arousing his anger, and not use it. Even though parents might wish their children could be more forceful toward others who might hurt them, teenage girls are very unlikely to be.

Openness, honesty and "I" messages are methods of communicating teens can use. ("I" messages use "I feel," or "I want," instead of "You are...")

Boys in turn need help understanding that rejection is a necessary part of the process of finding someone who genuinely likes them.

*"If a girl latches on to you and doesn't really
like you, only wants a boy friend, then you will have
a harder time finding someone who does really like
you. It is a dead end relationship but you are stuck
because no one else will approach you. And you'll be
spending your time with her instead of looking around.
It hurts when someone says, 'I won't go out with you,'
or 'I only want to be friends,' but it leaves the
door open for others."*

When boys complain about not knowing what a girl
really feels, they can be reminded that she may be
afraid of hurting his feelings. Girls need to be taught that
boys would rather have the pain of a straight rejection
than to waste time and energy on a relationship that
will never be.

Girls can be taught that feeling guilty may be a sign
of being pushed or manipulated. One standard line girls
can learn to recognize is "I like you so much; you
can't turn me down."

4. Stereotypes lead to different interpretations of dress.

Boys dressed in shorts, cutoffs, or shirtless are not
usually considered to be making any statement about sexual
availability. That could be because the male role requires that
they always be "ready." Girls' dress is judged as advertising
availability. Conflicts between parents and daughters often
result from the parents' fear of misinterpretation. Although
rape victims have traditionally been thought to have been
dressed "seductively," statistics say that rape victims are
dressed like everybody else, or even less well. But studies of
attitudes show dress to be one of the ways a boy judges
whether or not a girl is saying "yes" to sex.

Strategies

Exercise: Ask your sons or daughters how they interpret clothes. Do clothes say anything about who someone is? How much money they have? Rebellion against adults? Ask if they think clothes affect the impression they give others. What kind of impression do they want to give?

Parents need to discuss the confusion about what dress says. They can tell girls,

"Even though it isn't fair, boys may decide that you are 'advertising' based on what you are wearing. I agree you should be able to wear what you want to wear, and I don't think anyone has the right to decide for you, but there may be a risk in some clothes. I am really confused about this myself, because most rapes are planned ahead of time, and don't seem to be at all related to how people are dressed, but attitudes about 'asking for it' seem to be related to rape. How you dress should have nothing to do with risk, and certainly doesn't make you to blame if someone misinterprets you."

Boys should be told not to assume a girl is available for sex, based on how she is dressed. They can be told that dress may be misleading, and may even make them angry, but that acting physically, or bullying because of that anger isn't okay. It is okay to say, "I don't understand. I thought you were interested, but now you aren't?"

5. Girls want boy friends. Boys are pressured to "score."

Strategies

Emphasize other accomplishments besides popularity.
Parents can sympathize with teens who feel left out
if they don't have a boy friend or girl friend. They
can say that in the years to come, boys and girls will
begin to be interested in each other for broader
reasons than they are in junior high or high school.
    Girls need to know that sex should never be the
price for a relationship. And boys can be taught that
sex is not the place for "winning" or "competing."
Both boys and girls who are attempting to fight peer
pressure need support for being different. Parents can
offer rewards, expressions of approval, and family
activities to cushion some of the pain.
    Sometimes parents can help teens find a circle of
friends who share their values: a volunteer service
organization, a church group, an alternative school,
a summer camp.

6. *People interpret girls' and boys' sexual activity differently.*
    Girls who have sexual intercourse are called "loose,
promiscuous, or easy." Boys, even if they use force, are often
seen as "just being boys."

Strategies

    Parents can acknowledge the unfairness of this while
saying it does exist. It contributes to rape because
of the idea that once a girl has said "yes" she
can't say "no." Girls are held more responsible for
their own rape, if it is committed by a boy friend or
someone they already have had a sexual relationship
with. So although girls do have the right to say "no"
after they have had sex with a boy, they risk being
forced another time and being held responsible by some.

Parents can express their disagreement with this view — which condones rape under certain circumstances, and seems to hold the victim responsible — and suggest to their girls some second lines. For example: in response to ''You've done it before, so what's the big deal?'' one may answer, ''It's still my choice, and what I've done before doesn't have anything to do with it.'' Or ''I make a decision every time. Don't you?''

7. Stereotypes lead us to believe that girls are responsible for what happens sexually. Boys ''can't help themselves.''

So it is up to girls to stop sex. This is the most powerful rationalization for the use of force. Males in this society may learn that they have the ''right'' to sexual intercourse under certain circumstances. Some of those circumstances are: if she led him on, if he is sexually aroused, if she goes to his house, or apartment — those times when he can't be expected to ''help himself.'' Girls are taught the rule too, that men have rights, and if she makes a mistake, and is forced into sexual intercourse, it is her fault. Unfortunately girls don't know all the rules, or may view the circumstances differently, or be talked into ignoring what they know, and then feel stupid. For example most girls understand that going to a boy's house when no one is home may be risky. A boy may persuade her, though, that he just wants to show her a record, a book, a pet. She may go along, but once there, the guy may force her down, and say, ''What did you expect?'' Under those circumstances she will hold herself at fault, and so will many of her friends.

Strategies

Parents can explain how insulting to boys is the notion that boys can't help themselves, and that there is no

truth in it. They can go on to talk about how sexual
decisions should be a shared responsibility, not solely
the girl's. They can talk about how confusing it is
to have society say, "Force is never okay, except...."
Parents of both boys and girls can continue to talk
about the pitfalls of making assumptions about sex
instead of asking. They can ask, "What is an okay
way to get your partner to do something and when?"
Or point out that, "It is okay to ask, not okay to
lie." and "It is okay to talk about why you want to
do it, not okay to say, 'I'll hate you forever.' "
   Not all teenagers will follow the rules about
asking, and teens need some ideas about how to spot
a situation which may be leading to the use of force.
Parents can emphasize the need to pay attention to
low levels of fear or anxiety. Teens have difficulty
using feelings as indicators of being manipulated
because their bodies are giving them all sorts of
strange signals. The excitement and nervousness about
dating and boy-girl relationships sometimes creates
chronic nervousness. Even so, teens can learn to tell
those feelings from feelings of being in danger or
being taken advantage of. Parents can say, "You know
how it feels if we ask you to do something you think
isn't fair? Pay attention if you get that same feeling
out on a date, or with an adult."

8. *Stereotypes lead boys to take unnecessary risks with their*
own well-being to live up to an image.
   The toll of the male stereotype is particularly apparent in
relationships. It works against closeness, cooperation and
intimacy very directly. The male code is the generally
accepted societal definition of how men should behave. No

particular man holds all these values.

The code of behavior affects emotional life, and those emotional costs affect sexual interactions.

Male Code	Emotional Cost	Sexual Consequences
Act Tough	Must be tough at all costs under all circumstances.	Dependence on women for emotional closeness.
	May lose perspective and good judgement.	Competition ethic leads to concern for "scoring."
	Must take dares. Trouble making friends.	Toughness may lead to unwillingness to listen to girl's answer, and willingness to use more force to change her mind.
Hide Emotions	Hiding emotions hurts. Boys lose contact with feelings of tenderness, fear, sorrow or compassion.	Little awareness of his feelings or partner's. Focus becomes sex and performance. Causes inability to empathize with girl's feelings .

Male Code	Emotional Cost	Sexual Consequences
Earn Big Bucks	Means working long hours in jobs for money, not interest. Outside hobbies and interests disappear. Little time left for self or family.	Media says dollars buy expensive cars, clothes, entertainment and women, But no money, no women. Generates fear of only being liked for cars or money. Resentment over work may surface as "you owe me sex for all I do for you." Frustration and rage generated by poverty may be part of motivation of some rape
Get the right kind of job.	These jobs require drive, unwillingness to accept "no" for an answer, and using people.	Not accepting "no" means denying self and others that right. Bullying people into sex accepted. Sex may be taken as successful male's right.

Male Code	Emotional Cost	Sexual Consequences
Win at all costs.	Personal and moral sacrifices required. Little time for simple recreation and play. Fear of losing intolerable. Pain is to be ignored. What works is right.	Believes that "winners." get the girls. Fears of losing may lead to use of force to gain sexual contact. Winning becomes basis of sexual decisions. No empathy for the other person is allowed.

Strategies

Parents can suggest to boys alternative ways of defining oneself as a man. Parents may want to offer the statements below to boys as affirmations, or even as a possible code of ethics to counter sex role stereotypes. (Modified from "Guidelines for Men" from MTI Teleprograms poster *Setting Non-Violent Limits as a Man.*)

I can show my feelings and express my fears when I choose to.

I can ask for help when I need it and offer help when I think it is needed.

I can ask for what I want but know I cannot always get it.

I can choose not to fulfill others' expectations of me.

I can consider new ways of thinking, acting, and relating to people.

I can decide for myself who I want to be.

I can express my frustrations, disappointments, and anxieties.

I can take responsibility for my actions and not allow other people's behavior to push me into choices I do not want to make.

I can show my strength by choosing not to use force to get my own way.

Boys and girls need rewards for lonely choices. They need help being different when it leaves them feeling isolated. They will not always feel good because they "did the right thing." Parents can take them out for pizza when they make responsible choices, such as deciding not to go to the party at the house where the parents were on vacation, because they knew the guys had making trouble on their minds. (Sol Gordon's *Teen Survival Book* is a useful resource for teens and parents about how to deal with being different.)

Differences In Interpretations

The differences between boys' and girls' interpretations of situations and behaviors have been studied through attitude questionaires. In one study, for example, boys and girls were asked to respond to a list of five things a "guy and girl" might do together. They were asked to indicate if the situation provided a signal or cue that either the guy or girl wanted to have sex. The situations included going to a guy's home alone when there is no one home, going to a park or beach at night, going to a party where there are drugs or a party where the couple took drugs, and going somewhere together after meeting for the first time in a public place. They found guys interpret girls' actions as meaning they are interested in sex, far more than girls see either their own or boys' actions that way. One of the situations most open to misinterpretaion is if a girl goes with a guy to his home. Some guys interpret that to mean she is ready to have sex, and that she has lost the right to refuse.

In the same study, eight questions were asked about how a guy and girl might behave when they were alone together. *Talking a lot about sex*, *physical actions* (such as playing with the other's hair, tickling, wrestling, and prolonged eye contact), and *telling someone "I love you"* or saying the other is understanding, were the behaviors studied. Again, males saw all three types of behaviors as indicating sexual interest more than females did. Talking a lot about sex was seen as most indicating sexual interest, followed by the physical, and then the "I love you's."

Girls see relationships quite differently. They may not necessarily intend to signal willingness for sexual intercourse, but because of the difference in the way guys and girls interpret behavior, their behavior may be seen that way by guys. While sex educators suggest that teens talk about sex actively rather than "just letting things happen" as a method of making more responsible decisions, parents need to emphasize that some people will misinterpret willingness to talk about sex.

None of these differences between guys and girls would be so important if it were not for the findings about force. When boys and girls were asked, "Under what circumstances is it okay for a guy to hold a girl down and force her to have sexual intercourse?" eighty-two percent said there were never any circumstances under which the use of force was okay. However when they were given a series of specific circumstances to respond to, they became less absolute. The percentage saying "never" to all the items decreased to only thirty-four per cent. A significantly larger percentage of females (44%) as compared to males (24%) said force was never okay. Force was most often seen as acceptable when "a girl gets a guy sexually excited," and least often acceptable when "a guy spends a lot of money on a girl."

Here is a summary of the teen attitudes reported in the study:

Is it all right if a male holds a female down and forces her to engage in sexual intercourse IF:

	% saying "No"	
	Male	Female
He spends a lot of money on her?	61	88

	% saying "No"	
	Male	Female
He is so turned on he can't stop?	64	79
She has had intercourse with other guys?	61	82
She is stoned or drunk?	61	82
She lets him touch her above the waist?	61	72
She says she is going to have sex with him and then changes her mind?	46	69
They have dated a long time?	57	68
She gets him sexually excited?	49	58
She's led him on?	46	73

This series of studies was conducted at the University of California at Los Angeles by Roseann Giarruso, Jacqueline Goodchilds, Paula Johnson, and Gail Zellman.

Lessening The Influence of Sex Role Stereotypes

Parents can respect and encourage friendships between girls and boys. Guys and girls who view each other as friends are much less likely to take advantage of or exploit each other. Friendships can provide fun and affection and help teens be less dependent on dates for their sense of worth and belonging.

> *"When I was in junior high, I walked home from the bus stop with a guy my age. The little kids in the neighborhood walked behind us laughing and teasing about 'Gary loves Kathy.' I was so embarrassed I never talked to him again. I didn't even have a chance to find out if he was a nice person."*

Parents may not witness these scenes, but if they hear about them, they can encourage teens not to give up their friendly impulses.

Same sex friendships should also be encouraged. Girls especially have a tendency to leave their friends in the lurch when a boy "friend" appears on the scene.

To encourage friendships parents can:

- INVITE friends of either sex along on family outings.
- HELP CREATE alternative groups to the in-group when needed with activities like going for pizza, having a foosball, ping pong, or pool table in the basement, or giving a ride to the movies.
- SET THE STANDARD that plans with friends are not changed just because a guy or girl called and a date suddenly appeared.
- DEMONSTRATE with their own friends how one values

and takes care of friendships.

- INCLUDE in the family circle people who are friends with both parents or with the parent of the other sex.
- ASSUME a boy and girl are friends, not romantic interests, until told otherwise.
- ASK QUESTIONS about friends just as one might about a romantic interest. "What do you two like to do together?" "Does she or he have brothers or sisters?"

Parents who want their children to experience cross-sex and same sex friendships are working against strong societal influences. They need to provide their children extra support and preparation for being different. Teens who have good friends, and know how to be friends with both sexes are much less vulnerable to pressures to exploit another.

Male dominance, believes anthropologist Peggy Reeves Sanday of the University of Pennsylvania, serves its purpose. Rape prone societies often have histories of unstable food supplies, warfare or migration. Such rigors force men to the forefront to repel attackers and compete with others for scarce resources and land. A belief system that glorifies masculine violence and teaches men to regard strength and physical force as the finest expression of their nature, reconciles them to the necessity of fighting and dying in society's interest.

Sanday concludes that the way society trains its boys and girls to think about themselves and each other determines to a large extent how rape prone or rape free that society will be. She believes we can mitigate the damage our unconscious biases do by raising boys, for example, with more reverence for nurturance and less for violence.

"One must be careful," Sanday says, "in blaming men alone or women alone for the high incidence of rape in our society. In a way we all conspire to perpetuate it. We expect men to attack, just as we expect women to submit."

Chapter 8

Touch: Affection, Confusion, Exploitation

The ability to recognize and react to touch which feels bad or confusing is crucial to avoiding some sexual assaults. The family is an important place for children to learn to receive good touch, reject unwanted touch and question confusing touch.

Yet there are many barriers to the development of that ability.

Parents are being encouraged to touch their children more. One bumper sticker reads, "Have you hugged your kid today?" As children reach pre-teen years, however, the barriers to reaching out and giving a kid a hug increase. As children begin to physically resemble sexually mature adults, parents become unsure about what kind of physical affection is appropriate. This leaves teens more dependent on peers for touch, reassurance, and affection at just the time that those relationships are becoming confusing. "Skin hunger" — the need for affectionate physical contact — is often cited by experts as one of the reasons teens begin sexual activity before they are ready.

Much touch which goes on between peers is very mixed. It is uncomfortable because it is new, or because what is meant by the touch is not clear. Pre-teens spend much time hitting, pulling, stuffing things down each other's shirt and doing whatever else is handy for touching. Because touch is so confusing during these years, it is not enough to say, "Come tell me if anyone touches you in a confusing way," which is the place most parents choose to start sexual assault prevention. Parents need new approaches for talking about and modeling touch.

Even knowing that lack of touch makes children more vulnerable to sexual exploitation, it can be difficult to increase the touching or change patterns of touch within the family. Here are some of the barriers:

...fear of spoiling children;

...beliefs about how to treat children based on their sex;

...confusion about love and sex, touch and sex;

...parental backgrounds which included inappropriate touch, or no touch;

...society's message that all touch is sexual and is therefore dangerous or confusing unless between lovers;

...fear of incest;

...not liking the rebellious teenage person very much, despite loving him or her;

...fatigue with giving and receiving touch.

Because of the fear of incest and confusion about love and sex, much touch is suspect except between lovers or between mothers and babies. Variations of touch which express caring, sympathy, joy, and affection are being lost because of these sexual overtones.

Understanding and talking about differences between sexual and other kinds of affectionate touch can encourage physical affection to continue between parents and children as children grow up. The "grownup" world of sexual touch and romantic relationships is frightening and risky. Children need

permission to enter that world with their peers in
age-appropriate ways — hand holding, kissing, or petting —
and then come home and experience safe, nurturing touch
which is not risky, stimulating, or ambiguous. They need to
learn about and see love and affection as qualities separate
from and not coming only from romance and sex. Romance
and sex are wonderful between equals who enjoy learning
about each other and sharing the responsibility for the
consequences of decisions. They are potentially hurtful when
those conditions are not present.

   Clearly defining the difference between nurturing,
affectionate touch and sexual touch will allow all family
members to be more comfortable with touch within the
family. This is a necessary definition for teens facing peers or
dates who may say, ''If you loved me, you would.''
   Here are some suggested definitions:
   • *Nurturing touch* is comforting, non-stimulating and
done primarily for the benefit of the person being touched.
Examples are neck rubs, pats on the back, hugs of
appreciation, brushing another's hair. In nurturing touch, the
recipient feels no demands and is comfortable.
   • *Affectionate touch* is more equally balanced between
the persons touching. It expresses affection. Examples are
hugs, holding hands, rubbing shoulders. If it is nonsexual
expression it probably doesn't involve sexual parts of the
body, except between those who are already sexually
intimate.
   • *Sexual touch* most often involves the sexual parts of
the body. Although the toucher may gain sexual pleasure
from touching more ''neutral'' parts of the body, such as the
back.
   The recipient of unwanted touch of any type may feel a
sense of discomfort or obligation.

Another barrier to touch within the family is the belief that boys and girls need different touch. From birth, male babies aren't handled as much as female babies. Boys are expected to do without cuddling and comforting at a much younger age than girls. Many boys learn to be embarrassed about physical affection and to channel those needs into horseplay, fighting, wrestling, and sports. At the same time girls learn to receive attention and affection by flirting. Girls are cuddled and comforted within the family until they are much older than boys, but they also learn flirting can be a quick and effective way to get attention.

Incest is, among other things, a family problem of touch. One tool for helping a family within which incest has occurred is to define openly and clearly what kinds of touch are appropriate between family members and which are not. The second tool is not to allow secrets, especially secrets about touch.

Fear of spoiling children, fatigue, and parental backgrounds are other barriers to nurturing and affectionate touch within the family. Some children learn negative methods of getting attention. Breaking that cycle can be very difficult. Raising children, running a home, earning a living and just surviving sometimes take all the time and energy parents have. In addition, parents themselves may come from a background of limited family affection, or abusive touch within the family. Under such circumstances, increasing the amount of touch within the family can be an overwhelming and frightening task. For these parents the best strategy is to *talk* with their teenagers about touch, with the goal of clarifying the different kinds of touch.

A whole range of touch activities has developed as excuses to touch others without the intent being obvious.

Some of these forms of "incidental" touch may have resulted
from society's barriers to touching. Examples of these are:

For children - Tag, tickling, crying, pouting, play
fighting, combing, braiding each other's hair, drawing
pictures on each other's backs, leap frog, felt marker pen
"tattoos."

For teens - piling ten people in the car, kissing booths,
hip checks, dancing, flavored lipstick, hayrides, chain dances,
teasing, stepping on backs of shoes.

For adults - getting "friendly while drunk or high,
holiday greetings, chivalry.

While there may be nothing wrong with some of these
ways of getting touch, they may be unsatisfying or confusing.
Recognizing and talking about these activities as ways to get
touch helps clarify their significance.

Several other forms of touch between family members
are also important to recognize and discuss with your
teenagers because they confuse the issue of touch within the
family.

A teenage girl will sometimes take her father's arm as if
he were her date, or hang all over him as if he were her boy
friend. She may drape a hand on his knee or put an arm
around his neck. These gestures are difficult to understand.
They may be affectionate. They may show a need for contact
with the parent, for touch, or to experiment or practice new
"dating" behavior. What these mean depends on the context
— whether it happens in public or in private, and the family's
usual way of touching.

These gestures may be competitive, possessive, or
affectionate; they may create discomfort and confusion for
either parent. Even when discomfort is created, it is often not

talked about. A father may withdraw from the child, ignore the touching, ask that it stop, be flattered, or tolerate it with the thought ''Better me than a boy friend; she's too young for a boy friend.'' He may also take advantage of and exploit it to lead a child into sexual contact.

Mothers' reactions can include being pleased to see affection, pretending not to see, feeling jealous or competitive without understanding why, attempting to stop or redirect it, or tolerating the gestures out of the belief that it is better not to interfere in the father-daughter relationship.

Teenage boys may do similar things. Some mothers report that their boys seem to ''practice'' on them. Sons may ''accidentally'' brush against their moms' breasts or buttocks. Mothers are just as confused as fathers about what to do. If it were anyone else, she would ask that it be stopped, but because it is her son, she isn't sure what to do. Parents sympathize with their children's desire to practice risky moves before making them with a peer. They can empathize with a girl, growing into a young woman, who no longer wants to relate to her father as if she were still a little girl. Society doesn't seem to present any alternatives to the romantic model.

Setting Limits

So it is up to parents to establish appropriate kinds of touch. However, parents may be reluctant to limit or restrict children's touching, at least until they have some positive suggestions. Or parents may believe that any touch is better than none at all.

There are good reasons to set some limits. It is important to help teens make distinctions between kinds of touch. Clear limits on appropriate touch between parent and child makes that touch "safe." Affectionate touch can be enjoyed without fear or discomfort that it is leading anywhere inappropriate.

Allowing parent-child touch that looks like dating behavior reinforces the idea that the only way to get touch is within a romantic relationship. To avoid exploitation and assault, teens need to know how to meet those needs in other ways.

"Accidental" touch should be stopped because it is disrespectful. It is the sort of "hit and run" touching that is sexual harassment. While teenagers don't mean to be bothersome, they need to know that it is inappropriate and hurtful to the person receiving it.

If there is occasion to deal with issues of inappropriate touch in your family, you might say, "Please don't touch me like that. I would rather you gave me a hug, patted me on the back or gave me the 'high' sign." Or, "I feel very uncomfortable when you hang on me that way. It makes me feel like your boy friend. I'm your father. I would like it if we could just sit beside each other and enjoy the music."

Confusion about appropriate touch increases as teenagers' bodies mature sexually. Fathers often stop hugging their daughters when they begin breast development. Breast contact has sexual associations and is confusing when associated with one's own child. Mothers too may feel uncomfortable when their sons' bodies begin to feel more like a man's than a little boy's. Concerned about the sexual overtones, both mothers and fathers too often withdraw from physical contact altogether, leaving the developing child without comfort and affection from the other sex parent. Discussing different types of touch openly with your teens can allow everyone to relax and share affectionate touch spontaneously.

If you have decided that you would like to increase the amount of affectionate touch within your family, start by counting how often you touch family members in a positive, friendly way, with no demands attached. How often do you receive simple affectionate touch from others? Then set a small goal to increase the amount of touch. It can be as simple as giving a good-bye hug instead of a peck on the cheek, or reinstating an old family ritual. Sid Simon's *Caring, Feeling, Touching* (Argus Communications, 1976) has several good exercises for increasing the amount of touch within the family.

Sometimes in a desire to increase family touching, parents or children submit to hugs, kisses, or other touch they don't really want, because "we should be touching more." Everyone still needs choices about touch. In fact when you aren't liking your child much it is probably not helpful to force yourself to touch, but even in his/her most ornery stage there may be moments of respect and affection during which you can remind yourself to make physical contact.

Children need to be told that adults don't always want to give a hug and that it is okay to come back later and try again. Parents need to tell children that everyone, child or adult, has the right to refuse touch they don't want right then, and parents need to demonstrate doing that. Children will learn they can survive being turned down.

The family's job is to provide good touch, and to help children understand clear limits on touch, giving and receiving, and how to set them.

Young children can be told about good, bad, and confusing touch as a tool for recognizing situations which may be assaultive. That does not mean, however, that all touch which feels good is okay, or that children don't have to put up with some touch which doesn't feel good. The idea that touch which feels good is good leads into a trap.

*"I'm not always sure what is normal sex play and
what is abusive. When I found my ten year old lying
on his five year old sister and rubbing himself in
an obvious sexual way, I stopped him. He said, 'But
Mom, it feels good.' I didn't know what to tell him
until I thought about it and realized it's still up
to me to set the limits. And one of the limits is,
'It's never okay to use a younger child for sexual
pleasure.' "*

This same problem occurs with teenagers — sexual touch
may feel good but be unwanted. And most parents are
unwilling for teens to have sexual intercourse simply because
the touch "feels good."

The confusion about touch grows as the child does,
making it even more important to continue to talk to children
as they reach pre-teen and teen years. There are all kinds of
confusing touch during the teen years. Activities which
appear to be for one purpose may turn out to be simply
excuses to touch. Some touch hurts, but seems to be friendly:
the pat on the back that's too hard. Some touch is approved,
such as a kiss from an uncle, but feels wrong. If parents will
talk about this confusion, and limit their value judgements,
they will have many opportunities to help a teen talk about or
resist a situation he or she doesn't like.

Teen: *You know sometimes my friends and I all
pile in a car and it's only after I'm in that I
realize it's just an excuse for someone to get
close to a girl. But I don't end up where I want
to.*
Parent: *Same person beat you every time?*
Teen: *No, I just always seem to end up standing
there like a dummy, like it really is only a car
ride. Next time I'm jumping in first.*

Feelings Vs. Action

Parents can also make the distinction between feelings and actions. Rather than tell children certain feelings are not allowed, it is more helpful to say that while all feelings may be allowed, not all feelings can be acted upon. It is possible to choose how to act in response to your feelings. A teen who is very angry with someone is allowed certain ways of showing that anger. Society is clear about the distinction between being angry with someone and punching that person in the nose. Society is not as clear about the differences between being attracted to someone and acting upon that attraction. Advertisements, media and popular literature make it appear that if you are attracted to someone and don't act on that in a sexual manner, you are a fool, a prude, or worse.

Parents can help counter the pressure by being clear about the difference between feeling and action. Any touching may arouse sexual *feelings* even when the person involved is not someone with whom one would consider sexual *behavior* (a parent, sibling or friend). Though the feelings are normal, that does not mean that one should or wants to *do* anything. Feelings exist only within oneself. They are not good or bad, they just are. They do not require any action. Teenagers can be told that one of the differences between children and adults is the ability to recognize feelings, and to make decisions about how to act on those feelings, based on adult knowledge of right and wrong. (The failure to recognize the adult's responsibility is part of the way children blame themselves in cases of child sexual abuse.)

No Strings Attached

Another way to talk about touch is to talk about non-demanding touch or no-strings-attached touch. As sexual maturity is reached and media messages and societal confusion about sexuality and touch increase, teens and adults often experience touch only in the context of leading to further touching, and ultimately to sexual intercourse. Children and teens can be introduced to the idea that everyone needs no-strings-attached touch and that every relationship should have an abundant proportion of it. Parents should be aware of, and talk with their kids about, the confusion which exists about touch and sex in society and consequently in many people's minds.

Often children are teased because of that confusion.

Parent: *I notice you and Sarah don't hold hands*
  any more.
Child: *The kids at school teased us.*
Parent: *What did they say?*
Child: *Oh, ...you know.*
Parent: *It's too bad that people don't understand*
  that people can just like each other, be friends,
  and be affectionate without it having anything to
  do with sex. It isn't just your friends at school
  who are confused about that, I'm afraid.

And the early years of independence bring similar experiences of misunderstanding.

College Student: *I had an embarrassing situation*
  at school this fall.
Parent: *Oh?*
Student: *Yeah, I thought the boy my roommate was*
  dating was real nice. So when I saw the two of
  them, or even just him, I would go over to talk
  and be friendly. I didn't think I was flirting,
  but I would touch him on the shoulder when I saw

*him. I even gave him a big hug after we won our
big game. But you know what happened next?*

Parent: *Your roommate got mad at you.*

Student: *Yes, and I don't blame her. He broke up
with her, but even before he did, he made a move
on me. Then when he broke up with her, he called
me. What kind of person does he think I am?*

Parent: *People can be pretty confused about
touch. Some people assume all touch indicates
sexual interest.*

Student: *I guess you're right. There is this
other boy who makes me pretty uncomfortable when
he touches me because I don't know what he wants.*

Parent: *And you are probably right to be cautious. Not
many people give simple affectionate touch. It's
great you can. It's too bad it was misunderstood by
your roommate's boy friend.*

Within the family and outside the family, touch is a
source of confusion. It is most confusing when nobody talks
about it. The best of all possible worlds is for kids to have
enough physical affection in the family with appropriate limits
and the opportunity to talk about different kinds of touch.
There are some specific ideas parents can provide them —
such as clearing up the confusion about sexuality and touch —
to give them tools for understanding and making decisions
about situations outside the family, and reducing their
vulnerability to sexual exploitation.

Chapter 9

Uses And Misuses Of Sex

Sexual ethics and values are changing in American society. Sex is used and misused in a variety of ways, some of which require consent, some of which require lack of consent. While it is a simple enough task to tell our teenagers that rape isn't okay, telling them isn't enough. The word, "rape" still calls to mind a violent attack by a stranger. Parents can help make sense of confusing sexual interactions by talking about the ways sex is used and portrayed. Parents can teach their values about which uses of sex are legitimate, which they are uncertain about, and which are absolutely intolerable. It will be more helpful to talk about the uses and misuses of sex, and lack of choice in sexual assault, than to talk only about rape.

> In *Men on Rape*, Tim Beneke says, "If we are going to say that, for a man, rape has little to do with sex, we may as well add that sex itself often has little to do with sex."

A teen who understands that sex is used in a variety of ways is in a better position to recognize abusive situations, and who might be willing to hurt someone else, than one who believes there are only two extremes, rape and sex. Parents can help them gain understanding of the variety of uses and misuses of sex by talking about television and radio programs, newspaper articles, and interactions with friends.

Because sexual behavior is so complex, some basic assumptions are needed to make decisions about whether or not a particular use of sex is ethical. Here are some assumptions which may help teens avoid sexual assault:

• *The need for sex is not as straightforward as the need for food.* Like the need for food though, the need for sex can be misunderstood and changed. People often eat when they are not hungry, stuff themselves, or starve themselves, doing violence to their own bodies. In the same way sex is sometimes twisted, indulged in when there is no real desire, or used as a means to degrade others, or oneself.

• *Consent and submission are not the same.* Consent arises from mutual caring and affection. Submission comes from fear or lack of choice. Some uses of sex require lack of consent.

• *Sex is good or bad* depending on the ability of the partners to be responsible for their actions, whether or not genuine consent is present, and the particular circumstances. Individual family values determine these. For some families the only circumstance under which sex is acceptable is marriage. Others have other conditions, such as mutual caring.

• *Within some relationships the necessary equality for consent is not present.* Counselor/client, teacher/student, coach/player, parent/child, adult seducer/teen partner, are all unequal relationships. Only flattery or mild threats may be needed to achieve sexual contact under such circumstances.

This is an abuse of power and harmful to the less powerful partner.

• *Human sexual behavior is expressed in cultural terms.* Though based on biological need, the actual form sexual behavior takes is determined by cultural teachings about what is appropriate.

Here is a list of some common uses of sex:

...to reproduce
...to express affection
...to release tension
...to pursue pleasure
...to create bonds
...to prove identity
...to prove popularity or be part of a crowd
...to rebel against the family
...to sell things
...to earn money or luxuries, or to pay back a debt
...to establish power over another
...as an instrument of terror and oppression.

The range of ways sex is used and misused shows how complicated the values about sexual behavior really are. Sex is not often discussed in this way, yet children are exposed to many of these uses daily, in the media, or in stories they hear.

The list itself suggests some ways to talk about this with teens, and questions parents can ask to help teens understand. The list gives some perspective about the choices teens face. Teens whose parents have discussed the complexity of sexual behavior are more likely to turn to parents with questions.

Here is the list again, expanded with further information and examples:

- *Reproduction*. Some people believe the only legitimate reason for sexual intercourse is if the couple wants to have a baby or is willing to take that consequence. Lack of information other than this rule makes it more difficult for teens to form their own sexual rules. If they decide to ignore the original rule, they have little basis for choice. Consent isn't necessary for reproduction. It is not known how many teen pregnancies are the result of victimization or exploitation. Parents need to talk about pregnancy as one of the possible consequences of sexual intercourse, and clear up any myths their teens may believe (such as "You can't get pregnant the first time"). Teenagers need to recognize that anyone who suggests sexual intercourse without contraception when pregnancy is not wanted, is not considering the consequences. Sex without contraception should never be a test of love.

- *Expressing affection* for another is a use of sex. Consent must be present or the sex is hurtful, not affectionate. Someone who pushes another to have sex to "demonstrate" love is showing a lack of affection. There are many other ways to show affection: "You can hug and kiss, discuss your life goals, just be with each other, dance, buy each other presents, help each other study, take walks, give each other back rubs..."
Nurturing someone is a related use of sex. Healthy, affectionate touch based on genuine wonder and respect for the other person is nurturing. Sometimes a teen may be tempted to give in to someone and have sex because of feeling sorry for the other. Pity is not an affectionate reason to have sex. It assumes the other person is inferior. In fact, if that

person knew the reason for the sex, he or she might not
consent.

• *Release of tension* [*"need"*] is sometimes used by boys
as a reason girls should give in to them and have sex. Boys
and girls are taught to be very different in their "need" for
sex. Girls learn that a boy "can't help himself" once he is
turned on; boys learn that after a girl indicates a willingness
for sex, she "loses the right to change her mind." Parents can
suggest alternatives to sexual intercourse to discharge sexual
tension as well as make it clear that force is never justified,
even if a girl "teases." Some parents approve of
masturbation or other kinds of two person sex besides sexual
intercourse. Others suggest physical workouts, jogging, or
other interests.

• *Pursuit of pleasure.* Some people argue that sex is just
one of life's pleasures and, "if it feels good, do it." Although
parents are unlikely to recommend this as the sole guideline
for their teens, they may be unconsciously influenced by it, as
may their teens. Teens need to know sex is rarely as simple as
that. Sexual experiences have consequences, may create
bonds, create hurt feelings, influence reputations, and so on.
Parents need to give examples of what people need to
consider before having sexual intercourse. Parents can
suggest that teens ask themselves, "Is anyone going to be
hurt by this?"

> *"If a girl has just broken up with your best friend,*
> *he will be hurt if he learns you've taken up with her*
> *so quickly."*

> *"If a guy has sex with a girl just to have sex, then*
> *doesn't see her any more, she is going to be hurt."*

Teens can ask themselves, *"Am I willing to risk the consequences is something goes wrong? If I break up with him tomorrow, or the birth control fails, or our families find out?"* And *"How do I know my partner has consented? Am I just assuming it because she hasn't said 'no' or because she agreed to come home with me?"*

* *Bonds* are created by sex, sometimes regardless of consent. Teens may use sex in the hopes of creating bonds. ("If I go to bed with him, he'll be my boy friend.") Or they don't necessarily want bonds but they appear anyway.

"You can't break up with me, I'll tell everybody what we did."

Parents can tell both boys and girls,

"Sex creates bonds, and you may end up feeling trapped with someone you don't like anymore."

Sometimes a girl or boy may agree to have sex to "compete." A girl may feel that once she has sex with a boy, he will choose her over others. This seldom works out as expected. If the boy wants to have sex for reasons of power or conquest, once the girl gives in she's not a challenge any more. She may feel horribly cheated. A girl may push her boy friend to have sex with her in the hope that it will be harder for him to break up with her, and sometimes it is. Consent may have been present, although it may have been part of a false bargain. A boy may feel that once a girl has had sex with him, she is his. The expression "having a woman" is sometimes used to mean sexual intercourse. Parents can make it clear that people may possess chairs, pets, or photos, but not people.

• *To prove identity*, or sexual attractiveness, is one way people use sex. Consent is not necessarily needed. Ask teens if they know anyone who flirts just to prove attractiveness or for the sake of the chase. Or others who seem to be interested only in "scoring" and not in the person.

• *To prove popularity or be part of a crowd* a teen may agree to sexual behavior. Teens may feel pressured by their peer group to have sexual intercourse, to be part of the gang, to have experiences to share, or because everyone else is. This pressure to be part of a group can be so strong that lack of consent is ignored. Gang rape sometimes involves this pressure. Parents can talk about group pressure, acknowledge it, and do everything they can to support teens' independence.

• *To rebel against the family* teens sometimes become sexually active. Rebellion against parental values is a natural part of being a teenager. Some choose sexual activity as a way to fight back at their parents. Others are victimized within the family and break away by forming relationships with peers or others outside the family. Sometimes teens from troubled families victimize others. Teens can be told that sex rarely cures problems, and often adds to them. They need to know they are more vulnerable to victimization when they are not getting along at home and that "help" with a sexual price tag is too expensive.

• *To sell things* is such a common use of sex, it's easy to overlook. "If you own this car, beautiful women will chase you." Teens need to feel attractive and frequently feel they need outside help. It is easy for them to want magic. Sex becomes a commodity, the "free gift with every purchase." Continued exposure to ads influences ideas about attractiveness. It is easy to begin to believe that the owner of a new sports car is more attractive than the owner of an old car. Ask teens about the content of the ads: "Do women only like men with new cars, or who wear a certain aftershave? Do you really think the girls you admire only like guys with motorcycles? Do you think guys like girls who wear makeup like that?" Parents can suggest other attributes about people to consider, like gentleness and a sense of humor.

• *To earn money or luxuries, or to pay back a debt* is a use of sex parents are unlikely to associate with their own children. Parents may even have warned their teens that "bargaining" with sex is risky. Jobs or money for independent spending are very attractive to teens. An adult may promise them something without strings, then add sex as a condition. By then the teen has some investment in the job or easy money, and has a hard time saying no. Teens need realistic guidance about the risks of trading sex for any material gain. Frequently such bargains are unspoken, one-sided, and rarely kept. No one has the right to request sexual favors as part of a job. If the partners aren't equal the bargain is exploitive.

Runaways are easily exploited and often offered a place to sleep and food in return for sex. Although parents may blame the teen, adults who take advantage of troubled kids are really taking advantage of a child's weakness. Prostitution and child pornography rings are an extreme form of this. Teens who become prostitutes have often been previous victims of sexual assaults, incest, or rape.

• *To establish power over another person* is also a misuse of sex. Rape is sometimes used as a method of control:

"I'll show you who's boss."

"I've taken your flaunting yourself as long as I can."
"You can't do this to me any more."

are all phrases rapists have used.

Degrading or humiliating another person is one of the ways sex is sometimes used to gain power. The first opportunity parents have to explain this one is when kids ask about the word "fuck."

"What does the F-word mean?"

"Do you mean how come it's used the way it is?"

"Yes"

"Well, that's one of the most confusing things about sex. It can be both wonderful and awful. Sex between two people who both want it can be nice; forcing sex on someone humiliates and hurts them. So 'F—- you' is saying, 'I want something mean and humiliating to happen to you.' "

OR

"What does it mean when someone says, 'When you get a little older I'm going to f--- you?' "

(Gulp. Avoid saying, "Who on earth said such a thing to you?")

"Could you tell what he meant?"

"No, It sounded mean. But isn't that something that two people who are going together do?"

*"Sometimes people who care about each other have sex,
but they don't usually say those words to each other.
Sounds like maybe this guy was kind of threatening.
Did it sound that way?"*

*"Yes, it scared me, but I was sort of pleased he might
be interested in me. I was only in the third grade. How
can you tell if a boy is interested in you?"*

Television and newspapers have plenty of horror stories
about rape. Teens tend to focus on the truly strange and
bizarre incidents. Parents can help teens understand that
even someone they know may be capable of hurtful acts.
Parents can try to bring them back to reality by discussing the
everyday qualities of the people in the news: "Do you think
this rapist in the paper has a girl friend, a mother, father,
friends? Do you think they are as weird as he is? If they are,
where do you think a whole group of weird people like that
might live? Do you think his neighbors are shocked?"

Using sex to blackmail or expose another is another way
sex is used to gain power and control. Teens are sometimes
emotionally blackmailed, "If you break up with me now, after
we have had sex, I'll tell everyone what we did." Teens are
frequently blackmailed into sexual contact. Young teens are
more afraid of getting into trouble than anything else. Even
though it is hard for adults to understand, an older teen or an
adult can give a teen beer or some marijuana, and then use
the threat of telling parents or the authorities to gain sexual
contact. Teens can be warned that others might try to take
advantage of them by getting them to break a rule. But even
being in trouble with the law is preferable to rape.

The power and control of sex is also used to to "initiate"
teens into a club, or bring them into a stable. In some sexual
abuse rings, the abuser gets the teens to go along with some

marginal sexual activity (such as strip poker), then uses the threat of telling about that to get further compliance with demands. Sometimes the victim goes along out of fear, a desire to be part of the group, or for money. Once having gone along, teens often can't find a way back out. To avoid feelings of powerlessness, victims sometimes confuse their own submission with true consent.

It is important to help teens believe that bailing out when a situation escalates, no matter what they have agreed to up to then, is the only way out. Parents need to emphasize that *true consent is not possible in relationships of unequal power.* Parents can say that they want to help even if their teens have made mistakes they are ashamed of. With younger teens, parents can be alert to the signs which indicate sexual assault may have occurred. With older teens it may be tougher to break through the defenses of the peer group, but it still may be possible to offer a way out.

To get revenge is another way sex is used, either against a woman herself, or "her" man. Teens see this in movies about the Mafia, gang wars, or in old cowboy shows. They are unlikely to encounter it in real life, although in a mild version a young woman might find an enemy of her boy friend paying extra attention to her, as if to steal her away. The interest really isn't in her, but in getting back at her boy friend. Unless someone has explained to teens this use, they won't understand it when they encounter it in life, or in the movies.

• *As a tool of oppression and terror* is another way sex has been used. The folk version is "keep her barefoot and pregnant." Minority women have been targets of this use, particularly during the time of slavery. Rape and torture are part of terrorist actions in many countries. Acknowledging this extreme negative use of sex can help teens understand the range from sexual violence to sexual activity. Talking with parents about this can save teens much of the bewilderment experienced when such a misuse of sex is recognized.

The physical act of sex is neither good nor bad. It is the equality of partners, the circumstances, the ability of both partners to give consent, the presence of consent, the use or absence of force and responsibility which determines whether a sex act is positive or negative, whether a healthy use or an exploitive misuse of sex.

These labels, or others, for the ways people use sex can help teens and parents understand particular sexual circumstances better, and talk about it more easily. Teens want to know:

> *"Why would someone do something like that, rape someone, have sex with someone when they don't really like her or him?"*
> *"People use sex in different ways, some of them hurt others, some of them are healthy."*
> *"Like in what ways?"*
> *"Remember that movie we saw last night? In that, the men and women were being genuinely affectionate with each other."*

Chapter 10

Love And Work: Avoiding Abuse In Relationships

Sexual exploitation prevention includes more than just learning to be assertive, saying no, being aware, trusting feelings and acting on them. If sexual assaults are really to be prevented, then changes need to occur in some fundamental aspects of relationships, so that abuse is no longer tolerated.

Most abuse goes on within the context of relationships. Sexual harassment, acquaintance rape, incest, or sexual exploitation happen between friends, acquaintances, neighbors, family members, co-workers — people who are supposed to care and be worthy of our trust. In that sense, this entire book is about relationships. Since teens are actively examining the nature of relationships, it is vital to discuss sexual exploitation with teenagers in the context of relationships.

It's important for teens to know that even if abuse happens within a relationship, abuse is abuse. To help teens recognize abuse and exploitation, it helps to talk about what is okay — what's "normal" in relationships, what can be expected, and what is deserved. It is much easier for teens to recognize exploitation if they have a clear idea of what makes a desirable, satisfying relationship.

Two of the most important relationships in teens' lives are work (school) and romantic relationships.

Teens As Students Or Employees

Teens need to know that within the working world sexual harassment is commonplace. It is also a significant problem for many high school and college students, both from fellow students and from teachers.

Most teens are confused about sexual harassment. They think it doesn't happen very much, that women invite it, that it isn't really a big deal or very serious, or that it is a problem mainly for airline stewardesses or waitresses.

Teens need the facts; otherwise they are likely to be powerless if they are ever confronted with sexual harassment.

It is estimated that seven out of ten women will be sexually harassed in at least one work place or school setting. Most will not report the abuse, fearing negative consequences, or believing that they were somehow responsible for the abuse, or that they should have been able to "handle" the problem better.

From *The Minnesota Exchange,* Spring 1984.

What Is Sexual Harassment?

Any repeated and unwanted sexual attention (verbal or physical) ranging from advances, suggestive looks, jokes, innuendos to explicit propositions and assaults which cause discomfort to a woman and interferes with her job or school performance.

Behaviors such as:

…Staring or leering with sexual overtones

…Spreading sexual gossip

...Unwanted sexual comments
...Pressure for sexual activity
...Any unwanted physical contact of a sexual nature
...Being expected to submit to sexual contact as a
  condition of employment, promotion or for a grade
  in the class.
   Studies show:

• 70 to 90% of working women have experienced unwanted sexual attention on the job at one time or another.
• 91% of reported cases in one study were of verbal harassment although more than half also included forms of physical harassment.
• Women ages 16 - 19 seem to be the most frequent targets.
• Women of color and teens are over-represented in the victim population. Their lack of strong work histories and their concentration in positions of low status may be contributing factors. (From "Who's Hurt and Who's Liable," Sexual Harassment in Massachusetts Schools." Massachusetts Department of Education, Division of Curriculum and Instruction, Chapter 622 Project, 1385 Hancock Street, Quincy, MA 02169, 1983.)
• Sexual harassment occurs with great frequency in secondary and vocational schools, with serious effects on performance.
• Many teenagers and women respond to sexual harassment by leaving their jobs or school programs.
• Both men and women can be victims of sexual harassment. However, women are three times more likely than men to be harassed in the first place, and to suffer serious negative consequences as a result. One fourth of male victims and 97% of female victims are harassed by men. (*The Minnesota Exchange*, Spring 1984.)
   Victims of sexual harassment experience many of the same reactions as rape or sexual assault victims:

embarrassment, fear, anger, powerlessness, loss of self-confidence, reduced ability to do work, drop in school or job performance, moves to another job or school.

Some examples of sexual harassment:

"My daughter has been pretty upset ever since this incident at school. She was cornered and dragged into the boy's locker room by some members of the basketball team. They left her in the shower where guys were still showering. I think the guys on the team thought it was just a good joke."

"My son has a friend who is large-busted and it seems that she gets comments and jokes all the time from guys in her history class. It's getting so bad that my son says she doesn't want to go to class anymore. Apparently the teacher joins in too, so she can't go to him for help. She asked another teacher for help and she said that the boys were just trying to flatter her, and if she didn't make a big deal out of it, they'd stop."

"Dirty notes being found everywhere — in her locker, her books, her desk — were really wearing down my daughter last year. These older kids would write 'I want your body' or 'Come meet me at the store and I'll buy these rubbers for us' or 'Come to our party and be sure to bring the pill.' Then they started calling her on the phone at night with the same stuff. She was really getting scared. It got so she wouldn't walk home by herself."

"My daughter worked at the local movie theater
after school a couple of times a week. Her boss was
always grabbing her, pinching her, or some kind of
touching she didn't want. It was really annoying
her, but the night he grabbed her and kissed her
hard on the lips she could hardly think straight
to keep on selling the tickets. She was so angry!
She quit her job."

"My fourteen year old son went to the roller rink
with a group of kids. He was standing in the
galleries and two girls he only vaguely knew from
school came up behind him, reached between his legs,
goosed him on his genitals, and laughed.
Everybody else seemed to think it was really funny,
but he was terribly embarrassed."

Talking to teenagers about sexual harassment means
explaining to them what it is and what to do about it if it ever
happens to them.

Research has shown that our sons and our daughters
have very different ideas about what sexual harassment is,
and how it effects them. It's typical for boys to consider what
they are doing as "teasing" or flattery while girls may be
offended or frightened by the same action.

In a Massachusetts high school, some male students
wrote sexually abusive language on a girl's test paper after it
was returned by the teacher. The comments upset and
embarrassed her. She reported the incident to a sensitive
administrator who spoke with the male students. They
admitted to writing the comments. The situation was
resolved through consciousness-raising rather than
punishment. The boys simply had not considered the effects
of their actions upon the young woman. They considered their

behavior to be a form of teasing, which is very typical in high schools. However, when they were asked how they would respond to the same behavior if it had been directed at their girlfriend or sister, they were able to see their actions in perspective. (From "Who's Hurt and Who's Liable.")

Talking about similar instances in our own childhoods or adult lives can help to start discussion on this topic. Or a parent may ask "Do you know any stories like that from school? From work? What do you think harassment is? How is it different from flirting with someone?"

A group of Massachusetts high school students clarified the differences between flirting and harassment this way:

FLIRTING
...both like it and do it and it keeps on going like that
...a glance — you feel attractive and complimented
...if you know the person (depends on how you know the person and how they say it)

SEXUAL HARASSMENT
...male does it to a female (usually) and she doesn't like it and she can't stop it
...a look or a stare — you feel invaded, ashamed, naked
...hints — obscene, suggestive
...pinch, pat, grab

(From "Who's Hurt and Who's Liable)

Teenagers need to know what to do if they are ever sexually harassed. There are many possibilities, but the most important thing to know is that ignoring the behavior is unlikely to change it.

When sexual harassment occurs in the work or classroom setting, it's also not easy for a victim just to say "get lost." It's not possible to avoid a fellow student, a teacher, or someone at work. Many victims decide to tell someone what is happening and how the harassment is making them feel. Some teens decide to confront the harasser, verbally or in writing, in the company of an adult.

There are also legal options: the victim can file a complaint through the Title IX grievance procedure at school (where lack of an adequate grievance policy is in itself a violation) or with the employer. Complaints can be handled through a civil suit, or directed to the Office of Civil Rights or a local agency dealing with sex discrimination.

Teens need to know:
- sexual harassment is abusive
- it's important not to ignore it
- they don't have to put up with it
- while deciding what to do they can keep a record of each incident
- they can get help
- they can talk about it
- there are actions that can be taken to stop the harassment

Avoiding Abuse in Relationships

Some people think that they can excuse any behavior by saying, "I love you." But even in romantic relationships, abuse is still abuse. What keeps teens trapped in an abusive love relationship is the strength of the belief in romantic love.

The romantic ideal says that anything wrong in a relationship can be fixed with more love. The notion that romantic love is enough to heal all hurts and misunderstandings ignores the fact that girls and boys are raised and treated so differently as to be in two separate worlds.

Sexual intercourse gained through lies is sexual exploitation. But the romantic code is such that some boys feel it is okay to lie, because the girls "know" they are. Or boys don't understand why "I love you" is such a big deal, so they just say it.

He says he really loves her. Honestly, really *loves* her. How does she know if it's something he is saying to get her into bed, or if he says that to everyone, or if he is lying? The problem of course is that saying, "I love you," is easy but acting in a loving way requires considerable maturity.

Girls need different messages than just, "Sex is all right if you love each other."

Parents can help teens understand that love is a matter of behavior, not just words. "When you love someone, it means you treat that person well. What someone says is not as important as how someone treats you."

Loving someone means each person:

> ...Listens to the other person and his or her ideas
> ...Considers the other's needs
> ...Exchanges physical affection consistent with the
>   relationship
> ...Lets the other be first sometimes
> ...Takes care of herself or himself
> ...Feels comfortable
> ...Wishes to be with the other person
> ...Feels valued when with the other
> ...Values the differences between them

...Has some common interests, activities, or beliefs
with the other
...Remembers things that are important to the other
...Stands up for the other in difficult scenes.

Being "in love" is a wonderful state. It makes people
blind to shortcomings. It can also make people blind to abuse.
Whether or not being in love is a good enough reason to have
sex, all parents can agree that love is no reason to accept
abuse. Being "in love" ends regardless of whether or not the
relationship does. Loving doesn't have to, if it is based on
more than fantasy.

Talking about abuse is easier if parents talk about
the difference between being friends and being
exploited. Here are some examples an 8th grade
health class gave.

FRIENDS	EXPLOITED
Watching movies, tv together	Talking behind your back
Talking, laughing making loud jokes	When people make you feel sorry for them just so you give them something
Playing games together	
Drawing together, riding around on bikes, even walking	When they use you to do a fun thing
	When someone I have spent the night with stays at my house just so she can see the guy she likes.
Going on small day trips without parents, by bus to downtown	

IS THIS LOVE OR ABUSE?

If your partner ever does any of these things to you, you may want to consider whether it is love or abuse:
...tells anti-woman jokes, or makes demeaning remarks about women.
...treats you or other women like sex objects.
...gets jealously angry; assumes you would date or have sex with any available male.
...insists you dress more sexy than you want to.
...belittles your feelings about sex or relationships.
...says you're a cold fish; asks if you're against sex.
...withholds affection or sex.
...insists on unwanted or uncomfortable touch.
...calls you sexual names like "whore" or "frigid."
...forces you to do things you don't want to do.
...publicly shows interest in other women.
...has relationships with other women after agreeing to go steady with you.
...forces you to have sex with him or others; forces you to watch others have sex.
...forces particular unwanted sex acts.
...forces sex after a fight or physical abuse.
...forces sex when you are sick or when it is dangerous to your health.
...forces sex without birth control when a pregnancy isn't wanted.
...forces sex and hurts you physically.
...is cruel to you — sexually, physically or emotionally.

(Adapted from *Getting Free: A Handbook for Women in Abusive Relationships*. Ginny Nicarthy, The Seal Press, 1982. Used by permission.)

Parents find it difficult to think about their teens being seriously abused within a relationship. Nevertheless, it does happen. Teens will be able to identify abuse more easily if parents have labeled abusive behaviors. The box on the preceding page gives a number of examples of behavior, some of which are extreme, others so common it is difficult to see them as abuse. Parents can use those in conversations depending on the age and relationship of their teens.

Although boys are much less likely to be abused, they are exploited and sometimes pressured about sex. Parents can modify some of these statements for boys. For example:

...is only interested in you when you have money.
...says you're a "wimp."
...belittles your feelings about sex or relationships.
...tells you not to worry if you ask about birth control.

It is necessary to *label* abusive behavior because of the "romantic code" under which girls and boys are raised. The differences are so great they have difficulty communicating with each other. And within a romantic relationship those differences create many opportunities for misunderstandings, anger, and abuse in the name of love.

THE ROMANTIC CODE

Girls Learn	*Boys Learn*
Love, sex and romance must go together.	Sex is okay without love or romance, although they may have to say they're in love.
They are responsible for how far sexual advances will go; they are responsible for stopping the advances.	They must make advances but face frequent risk of rejection.
They must balance pressures to be sexually "free" and liberated, but not earn a reputation for "sleeping around."	Men have lots of sex and lots of sexual partners; their sexual urges are uncontrollable.
If they say "yes" to sex, they are "easy." Must be "swept away."	They will have to coax and persuade to get sex.
They give sex.	They take sex.
They must be attractive but not too attractive or they will be called "seductive."	It's a real plus to be attractive, but not required for sexual success.
Their role is to be passive dependent, nurturing.	Their role is to be aggressive, tough, independent.

When girls become interested in boys, they are interested in romance, in having a boy friend. Boys seem to focus on girls because they want to explore sex. Young women may not want sexual intercourse. They want physical contact, affection or just someone to listen to them. Traditionally boys have been taught to ignore their emotional needs and to channel their needs for physical contact into athletic activities or sex.

Confusion results as boys and girls begin to interact in response to their interest in each other. They may have very little understanding of each other, and they generally lack the skills to communicate with each other. Not only may this be a setup for acquaintance rape or sexual exploitation, it often leads to painful and difficult relationships. Boys and men feel angry toward women because of the pull of sexuality. Women are the ones who say yes or no. Men see women as "flaunting their sexuality" while denying men access to it. Girls think boys hold all the cards in dating, relationships, and sex. But boys feel girls are the ones with the power.

Within the romantic code, girls are not allowed to be responsible for their own sexuality. This means they have difficulty expressing desire for sexual contact. They must be "swept away." This leaves boys guessing and often feeling that, even if they ask the girl what she wants, she won't answer honestly. This confusion, and the different consequences of sexual intercourse for boys and girls, cause serious problems. Boys and girls come to relationships socialized to want and need different things, and with different risks for choices made.

Patty and John have been going steady since they were freshmen. They are about to graduate from high school. Both plan to go to college next year in another state. They have been sexually active ever since they made a serious commitment to each other early in their junior year. When Patty discovers she is pregnant, she feels trapped, scared and unsure of what to do. She tells John, sure that they will be able to work out a solution. John reacts by insisting that she have an abortion, and saying that if she doesn't, he won't help. Patty realizes she wants to have the baby and thinks that she can talk him into changing his mind. John feels more and more trapped and departs for college leaving Patty pregnant and alone.

If one were to talk to John he would say that since he didn't plan to get Patty pregnant, he won't let it affect his life plans. He is able to walk away, maybe not without pain, and possibly not totally. Patty has no choice. Her life is already changed. She didn't plan to get pregnant either, but she is. She feels betrayed by her body and by John.

Even from this mutually agreed upon sexual intercourse, the consequences are enormously different for a girl than for a boy. A boy may well suffer too, for unplanned pregnancy, and many are more responsible than John. But this reality of different consequences for girls and boys is part of the fundamental difficulty in helping boys and girls understand and cope with romantic relationships.

Another example:

A girl and a guy are dating. She feels things are going well. He likes her. He's a nice guy. But then she finds out that her boyfriend is "one of the guys," telling each other who scored with whom, including details.

This is consenting sex which ends up being used by one partner in a way that is harmful to the other. Is that abusive? Certainly it is a betrayal of trust.

Some questions a parent could suggest a teenager consider to evaluate trustworthiness in a partner:

...Is she loyal?
...Does he treat me the same in front of friends as
    he does when other people are around?
...Does she ever share my secrets with other people?
...What does he say about past relationships?
...What have I heard around school about how she
    treated past boy friends?
...What does he say about his parents?

To help teens avoid sexual exploitation within a romantic relationship, parents can label abusive behavior, talk about love never justifying abuse, and help teens evaluate relationships. These methods are likely to be most effective before a teen is in a romantic relationship. Once "in love" teens — like the rest of us — don't want to hear anything negative about their loved ones.

About the only thing parents can do then is ask questions. Here is a list of suggestions. (Most parents will not want to ask all of them — especially not all at once — but any could start discussions.)

...How can a guy tell if a girl is interested in sex?
...How can a girl let a boy know she is interested in
    sex without being thought of as forward? Can she?
...Do you think girls ever have sex when they don't
    really want to?

...What about a guy? Why do you think they do that?

...Why do girls say no to sex if they really do want
to have sex?

...Why might a guy say yes to sex or even initiate
it even though he didn't want it?

The dialogue will end quickly if the teen feels tested, so
the best strategy may be for parents to throw information out
in the ''some people think'' form, or to add information with
''I think....'' The goal is to get teens to think about situations
before they happen, and question their own beliefs and those
of friends. Questions need to be phrased to protect teens'
right to privacy about their own sexual behavior.

More questions to stimulate discussion:

...How do you think a girl can tell if a boy likes
her if he doesn't talk about feelings?

...How do people decide when they like someone a lot?

...Have you thought about how people decide how far
to go with sexual activity with someone?

...Have you thought about how far people can go with
each other and still stop?

...Why do you think some people might think it would
be okay to threaten to hit a girl to have
sexual intercourse with her? What about if
she had already let him touch her breasts?

...If a boy spends a lot of money on a girl does
she owe him anything?

...Do you think it is okay to go out with someone you don't like?

...How come if a girl says yes, she loses her reputation, and a boy doesn't?

...Is being whistled at or having sexual comments made to you a good thing, or a bad thing?

...How can you tell if you are ready to make love with someone?

...How do you decide to trust someone?

...Whose fault is it if a guy slaps a girl around after she has let him in the house when her parents aren't home?

...Is it rape if you know the guy?

...How do you think alcohol affects people's ability to make decisions about sex?

Chapter 11

Family Stress: More Risk For Teens

In a recent study of teens involved in sexual assault, one factor which consistently distinguished victims from non-victims, and offenders from non-offenders was the number of family crises. In two out of three years of the study, both victims and offenders reported more disruptive events, such as divorce or extended unemployment, in their homes than did teens not involved in a sexual assault. This study also found an association between being a victim or offender and delinquent behavior in general.

Other studies have found that children in stepfamilies are sexually assaulted in greater numbers than children in intact families. Some research has linked alcoholism and sexual abuse. The connections between family situations and sexual assault have been found in enough research to deserve parents' attention.

The following factors are often disruptive to the family and may indicate particular vulnerability for teenagers. Later in this chapter we'll look at the major factors in greater detail.

- *Divorce.* In one study of teenagers of divorce, some of them preferred to hang out with the "wilder" kids because they didn't seem as naive.

Teens in divorced families may also be vulnerable because of the intense feelings generated by the divorce.

Often, because of the circumstances of the divorce, they cannot turn to either parent. They look to peers for support and comfort. Sometimes kids run away from home because of their anger and upset. Runaways are very vulnerable to sexual exploitation.

• *Remarriage.* Children with stepmothers are more likely to be assaulted. Stepfathers are over-represented in the figures on sexual assault within the family. Fathers and step-fathers are named as offenders about equally in intrafamily abuse. But there are fewer stepfathers than fathers in the population, so stepfathers seem to represent as additional risk to kids.

• *Single parent families* can be as stable as any other family form, but initially the crises which led to single parenting and the stress of resettling may produce greater vulnerability.

• *Alcoholism.* Research on children of alcoholics is limited but seems to indicate many factors which might leave a child unprotected or more vulnerable. Incest has been called the closet problem of alcoholism. One-third of all sexual assaults involve the use of alcohol.

• *Battering.* The unspoken part of physical violence is sexual violence. Teens who come from a family in which battering takes place have to be considered at risk to victimize others, or to be victimized.

• *Sexual assault of parents.* There is a some evidence that children whose parents have been sexually assaulted seem to be more likely to be assaulted themselves. Some men who were sexually abused as children sexually abuse children. On the other hand, parents who have been sexually assaulted seem to be more likely to talk with their children about avoiding sexual assault.

- *Extended unemployment* has been linked to many family and personal difficulties. Feelings of worthlessness, depression and fear generated by extended unemployment may increase the likelihood of abuse. Kids from these families may see more violence, or more alcohol abuse, which may cause them to seek comfort or release outside the family. Extended unemployment is also named as one of the stress factors leading to intrafamily sexual assault.

Race is sometimes identified as a factor of vulnerability. Most studies find few differences based on race. One study found that black females were more likely to be violently attacked but no more likely overall to be sexually assaulted.

None of these life circumstances is rare. Although they may increase teens' vulnerability, there are measures to help teens facing these circumstances:
    ...Talk to them about what is going on.
    ...Make extra efforts to include them in family
        activities and projects.
    ...Get outside help early, before the situation
        has progressed too far. Once serious sexual or
        physical abuse has occurred in the family,
        legal action is likely once the abuse is
        discovered.
    ...Get help for yourself so that you have more
        energy for your children.

Divorce And Remarriage

Although divorce represents a very difficult crisis for everyone in the family, the opportunities to talk about marriage, sex, relationships, love, and caring between adults and children should not be ignored. It is a good time to say that people have the right to be treated well, and an obligation to compromise those rights only so far before relationships should be ended.

While children are trying to understand a divorce they may ask how people decide they love someone, and how people decide to marry someone. Older teens might benefit from some honest answers, instead of being given just those which protect mom's or dad's character. Instead of, "Your mom is a wonderful person, we just didn't get along," an answer could be, "I felt obligated, even though I was afraid it wouldn't work." Or, "People were expected to get married so I didn't even question it." Or "He was a wonderful person but as I got older I wanted different things and he didn't."

Children almost always want to get their parents back together. They may ask, "If you and Mom are still friends, how come you don't get back together again?" The question can lead to an explanation that being friends with someone is much easier than being lovers and/or living together, and that sometimes it is just much better to be friends.

"If you're not married to Dad anymore, how come he cares if you date?" provides a chance to talk about love, possession, and jealousy. It may be a good time to say that jealousy is not a true test of love.

During the divorce transition period children are often exposed to new people as the single parent makes new friends or begins to date. The newly single parent is often vulnerable, questioning values and actions never doubted before. She or he may be less able to resist manipulation than at more stable

times. Child care arrangements often change as they often do
again after remarriage. All these events increase the risk to
the children.

When a divorce has occurred because of alcoholism,
battering, or sexual abuse, protecting the children may
become more difficult. The abuser may demand to see the
children, and be able to get a court order to do so. The
children then are without the protection of the other parent.
This is one of the most frustrating situations for all those
interested in protecting children. Sometimes the best
custodial parents can do is be very specific about their
willingness to help, and be available to help the children
without ranting and raving about the other parent.

Stepfamilies

Children in stepfamilies, especially teenagers, are at risk
for sexual abuse and for unwanted sexual activity for several
reasons.

• Children in stepfamilies do not seem to be as well
protected. They are frequently with people who are not
related to them, and not bound by the "incest taboo."
Stepmothers may be seen by others as having less authority
and less ability to provide protection.

• Children in stepfamilies frequently have stepsiblings of
the same age. Brother-sister incest is common. Without help
from parents, stepsiblings may not know what limits to put on
their behavior. The complex emotional stew of competition,
jealousy, feeling left out of the new adult relationship, and the
increased sexual atmosphere in the new couple relationship
may set the stage for abuse. Children and young adults need
explicit discussion about appropriate sexual behavior within
the family.

- Children in stepfamilies face separating from their parent sooner than children in intact families. They often turn to their peers for approval and affection. If they do not have good independent decision making skills, they may be more susceptible to peer group pressure toward sexual activity. Sometimes an element of ''Mom and Dad are doing it, but not with each other,'' may be an excuse.

- Children in stepfamilies are frequently able to manipulate their custodial parent into not setting limits. The teen may say, ''If you don't let me do it, I'm going to go live with Dad (Mom).'' The parent may give in rather than risk that confrontation. Most teens will follow reasonable limits, however, if the limits are clear and consistently enforced.

- Older teens in a stepfamily may separate from their family before they are really ready. They are headed in a different direction than the parent-stepparent couple. The newly marrieds want to form a family. The teen is breaking ties. Rather than learn how to get along in this new family, the teen may simply leave.

- Competition between young adult stepchildren and the same-sex stepparent, (or same-sex parent) can get very complicated. An unethical adult can use this as an excuse for sexual abuse. An adult moving into a stepfamily should be prepared to set verbal limits with a teenager about touch. (Refer to Chapter 8.)

- The common advice given stepfamilies about sexual behavior is to be discreet about physical affection between new partners. Another more direct approach would be to express clearly the notion of special affection between adults which does not include kids. Children need that message "loud and clear," and to have it repeated in both reassuring and limit-setting ways. At the same time, the appropriate affection between parents and children should be emphasized as well.

• Custody disputes may leave children unprotected. Because there is often so much bitterness and anger during divorce and custody settlements, charges of sexual abuse are less likely to be believed than usual. Women are suspected of setting their children up to lie about the situation. However this is one of the times of life when children may well have been sexually abused. Because parental rights are considered so strongly, and sexual abuse is so difficult to document, a parent is rarely denied visitation rights. Sometimes visitations are to be supervised, perhaps by the new wife or a grandparent. Neither is likely to believe charges of sexual abuse, nor to provide adequate supervision.

Teens may also be disbelieved if they accuse a stepfather of sexual abuse. The teen may be seen as jealous or attempting to get rid of the stepfather. Teens are unlikely to lie about such an offense.

• Non-custodial parents may drift into sexual contact out of loneliness and unsureness about how to express affection. They inadvertently ask the child to fill in for the spouse who is no longer there. Without the normal constraints of family life, sexual abuse may occur. If confronted, however, this person will often be anxious to change the offensive behavior.

• Stepfamilies are usually unable to monitor their children and the people around them as well as intact families. Children in stepfamilies often visit another household every other weekend and/or for extended periods during vacations. From these households, the children often visit or are visited

by yet another set of friends and relatives with an unknown
set of values and goals for children. The rules in the other
household are usually different, leading to even more
confusion about when a child has some power and when "no"
is an acceptable response to a question or request.

• Loyalty binds can make it unlikely, even when they feel
abused in the other family, that children will say anything
about it. Children in stepfamilies sometimes don't want to
hear or acknowledge anything negative about the absent
parent. They are afraid of getting the parent in trouble or of
being restricted from seeing the other parent. It takes a very
strong combination of information and skills for the children
to even know where to turn if something does happen to them.

Some of the questions children ask during the formation
of a stepfamily provide opportunities to talk about these
issues.

"Who do you love better, me or [the new stepparent]?"

This is an opportunity to explain different kinds of love. Love
for a child is and should be different from that felt for an
adult.

*"You kiss and hug all the time and you never did
that with Mommy. Now she's all alone and lonely."*

This comment offers an opportunity to talk about stages of
relationships and the fact that kissing and hugging are signs
of affection which no longer existed in the old relationship.

*"But if I told you that Mom's new husband did
anything to me, you would never let me see Mom
again."*

If a teenager says this the response can contain, "You're old enough to decide about seeing your mom yourself. I would still like to be able to help you with problems, when I can."

Single Parent Households

The limited time and energy of any one person can create extra difficulties. Single parent households often lack the back-up of another adult within the household to ease the load of parenting.

Most single parent households are headed by women, often without adequate income. This means that single-parent households have several factors making it more difficult to provide protection and limit setting for teens.

Perhaps the best possible approach for a single parent is to use the "We're all in this together" problem solving method:

Mother: *"I would like your help with a problem."*

Kids: *"We've been trying to do our share around here."*

Mother: *"Yes, I know and I appreciate it. But this is a new problem for us. You are starting to get to the age when kids are going to pressure you about lots of different things, drugs, sex, rock and roll... I'm worried that I'm not around enough to supervise you and I want to be sure that we all agree about some of these things."*

Kids: *"What about rock and roll?"*

Mother: *"You know I was kidding, but what about drugs? And I am concerned about people pressuring you to have sex, or to take advantage of someone else. And since I'm not home, I might never know."*

Kids: *"You know there are lots of mothers who
aren't home."*

Mother: *"I know, I guess I just feel responsible since
we're on our own. Can you help me feel more secure
about this whole thing?"*

Kids: *"Well, if it helps, no one has pushed much
more than a little pot at our school. But you're
right, the kids are necking, and you can't always be
sure what is going to go on at parties. But don't
you trust us?"*

Mother: *"Yes, I just want to be sure I've been clear about
how I feel about early sexual activity."*

Kids: *"You're against it...."*

Mother: *"Yes, that's right. At least we have that part.
Do you agree?"*

Kids: *"Yes, but you know I'm not sure how good I am at
telling kids no."*

Mother: *"Maybe we could practice that. Could we set
aside a time every week when we can talk about what
is going on, and we can practice? You know, I could
use some practice saying no too."*

Kids: *"Yes, but when? You're always busy."*

Mother: *"Well, this is important to me. How about
Saturday morning? That doesn't interfere with any
of your activities, does it?"*

Another problem faced by single parents is dating. Sometimes girls will compete with their mother (and sometimes mothers with their daughters) for boyfriends. A man willing to exploit the situation can abuse the teenager, and blame her.

As difficult as this is to talk about, single parents need to be aware that someone they date might be willing to exploit the situation.

The best protection is to have talked very specifically to your children about sexual assault. In this case that might go something like this:

Mother: *"If any of my dates approaches you in a way you don't understand or one that seems sexual to you, please let me know. I know that it might seem flattering if someone older than you approached you sexually. Of course I will try not to bring home anyone who might do that, but it isn't possible to tell by the way someone looks, or even by talking at first. If any of my dates asks you to keep a secret, that should be a warning too, that he is up to something no good."*

Teen: *"But what if I like him?"*

Mother: *"Well, I know it might be tempting to go along with him, but how would you trust someone who came here with me, and then decided to switch to you? How would you ever know where you stood with him?"*

Teen: *"Well, all right, so I told you. How do I know you'll believe me and won't just think I'm jealous or want you to break up with this guy because I don't like him?"*

Mother: *"I promise I will try to listen, If I don't listen very well, I give you permission to tell someone else. Who could you tell?"*

Teen: *"How about Dad?"*

Mother: *"Well, he certainly wouldn't be my first choice. There's still some unfriendliness there. Isn't there someone else?"*

Teen: *"I thought you would say that; I was just checking. What about your sister?"*

Mother: *"That's a good idea. Okay, we know what we're talking about, right?"*

Teen: *"Right."*

A single parent usually has less money than a two-parent family. Talking with a teen about how it is harder to be safe with less money, and that it can be tempting to take greater risks like hitchhiking, can lessen some of the risk.

Having to count on other people to help with things like fixing a car, repairing a broken furnace, and carpooling creates a pool of people who are known to parent and children, but whose basic trustworthiness is unknown.

A problem faced by many women is feeling obligated when a man helps with a household chore, and then feeling betrayed when that sense of obligation is used to gain sexual contact. Kids are vulnerable to this same pressure, but can be helped by talking about obligations not leading to sexual contact.

"If someone wanted you to have an obligation to them, they should state the bargain ahead of time, and if the bargain includes any kind of sexual act, then it isn't a fair bargain."

Hitchhiking is one danger most parents fear, but boyfriends can be an equal problem. A teen girl may be worried enough, or tired enough, of trying to get around that a boyfriend with a car can seem an attractive alternative. The price may be sexual activity before she is ready. Talking about that ahead of time will work better than saying, "I don't like your boyfriend."

Mom:*"I know it is tough getting around and always having to depend on your friends. Have you thought about wanting a boyfriend with a car just so you would always have a way to get around?"*

Teen: *"I wouldn't do that. Besides, I don't know any boys with cars."*

Children Of Alcoholics

The use or abuse of alcohol by a family member can increase the risk of sexual assault.

• Alcohol is involved in one-third to forty percent of sexual assaults. Men use alcohol as an excuse for behavior they would not tolerate otherwise.

• Children of alcoholics suffer from a crazy family pattern. They learn several false notions from the alcoholic interactions:

...They are responsible for the other person's well-being.
   (A set-up for the "You'll make me so happy" line.)
...They must "take care" of the other person.
...They must be submissive to avoid upsetting the
   drinker.
...They must not talk about the family situation.

• Children of alcoholics often suffer physical or emotional
deprivation, regardless of socioeconomic class. This can leave
them inadequately supervised, uninformed about touch, and
needing nurturing contact.

• Children in alcoholic families suffer from low
self-esteem, which may be linked to abuse and to early sexual
activity.

• Children also may be looking for a way out of the house.
For girls, a boyfriend may be an easy option.

• Alcoholic families are often isolated due to shame and
embarrassment. This also leaves children vulnerable.

• When bad things happen to children they assume they
did something to deserve it, or that they are bad children.
This leaves children in alcoholic families vulnerable to abuse,
and harder to teach that they don't deserve mistreatment.

*   *   *

Twenty-five million children under the age of 11 live in
homes where they are sexually abused. Incest occurs in many
homes of all classes. Most victims are initially approached
between the ages of five and eight, with the incestuous
activity usually continuing for a minimum of three years.

While research about incest and its relationship to alcohol abuse is limited, and varies in its conclusion, a number of studies document that over fifty percent of known incest victims lived in homes where alcohol abuse was a major problem. In addition, many therapists report sixty to eighty percent of the alcoholic women they treat were once incest victims. One clinician's research indicates twenty-six percent of children in alcoholic homes have been incest victims.

While many children in alcoholic homes do not experience direct sexual violation, many others nonetheless relate the fear of possible sexual abuse. Others may feel an unexplainable shame about their own sexuality.

The best things parents in an alcoholic household can do for their children are to talk about alcoholism and to join a support group for themselves. The healthier parents are, the more help they can be to their children. Instead of ignoring the risks to their children, recognizing and discussing them can undo some of the damage. Parents can try to find other trusted adults for their children to look up to and gain acceptance from. Often just one person who believes in a child will keep that child going.

As parents inform children about the disease of alcoholism, they can make sure the child understands that:

...no matter what the accusations of the alcoholic, drinking behavior is not linked to the child's behavior.

...it is not necessary to forgive parents before they are ready.

...alcohol is no excuse for an adult to commit sexual abuse. (Although due to alcoholic blackouts, alcoholics may honestly not remember perpetrating abusive behavior.)

As parents get healthier, they can develop activities for themselves and their children which will increase their sense of competency and worth. This can combat some of the low esteem that the actions of the alcoholic created.

Alcoholic mothers often blame themselves if their child is sexually assaulted. While there may have been inadequate supervision, the offender had to be willing to commit what is to most an unthinkable act to turn neglect to disaster. Guilt is only useful if it propels one toward new behavior.

Activities for parents and children can decrease their sense of isolation, whether the activities are through church, one of the support groups for children and spouses of alcoholics, or a group based on some other interest. Spouses of alcoholics sometimes become isolated out of shame. Breaking that pattern is necessary for the health of the children.

> *Alcoholism may be the most unidentified disease in our society. Estimates are that one out of ten people who drink alcohol are physiologically alcoholics no matter what stage of the disease they are in.*
>
> *The myths about alcoholism may prevent recognition situation of danger, just as the myths of sexual offenders in general lessens recognition of risky situations.*
>
> *The average alcoholic is a man or woman somewhere in the middle thirties with a good job, a good home, and a family. [Less than 5% of alcoholics are on Skid Row.]*
>
> *All these facts taken together mean that everyone has a very high likelihood of knowing families in which alcoholism is a major element.*
>
> *Any suspicion that someone who has responsibility for children may have an alcohol problem, is cause for concern and gathering further information about the disease of alcoholism. In addition to the link to sexual assault, it is probably the number one killer in this country.*

Sexually Assaulted Parents

If you were sexually assaulted as a child, it is more likely that you have already started talking to your own children about sexual assault. There are a number of issues to consider. First, what effect does the sexual assault still have on you? Do you have some lingering self-esteem issues, or guilt, or fear? Was the sexual abuser someone in the family, still around in the role of a grandfather, uncle, or other relative in contact with your children? How might that earlier sexual abuse influence your choice of male partners? Was the sexual abuse connected to alcohol use or abuse?

You need answer these questions only to yourself, but you may find it valuable to write down the answers, talk to a friend, or seek one of the agencies which works with adult victims of child sexual abuse.

If you have taken care of yourself, and the problem is that the sexual offender is in the family, then you need to know that sexual offenders don't change without outside intervention and that it is possible that the person will also victimize your children.

Battering

Teens who grow up in a family in which battering occurs are at risk of sexual assault both within and outside of the family. Children who are sexually or physically abused may sexually abuse others. Outside professional intervention is necessary to change a battering situation. No one within the situation can change it alone.

There is no quick and easy solution for a family in which battering occurs. There are resources to help women sort out their options. The one thing which is clear is that staying with the batterer for the sake of the children is not necessary or likely to be in their best interests.

Teens from battering homes need the same messages as children from alcoholic homes:

- What happened to them was not their fault. They did not deserve the beatings or abuse.
- It is not okay to use violence on other people. There is no excuse for it.
- There are alternatives for achieving what one wants, or expressing anger and negative emotions.
- Breaking the secrecy, shame, code of silence, and isolation which the batterer creates is the first step toward help.

Extended Unemployment

Several factors may be involved in the added vulnerability of teens in families where extended unemployment is a crisis.

Sexual abuse within the family appears to increase during periods of extended unemployment. This type of abuse is called "stress-induced." Men who are unemployed may suffer from depression and diminished self-esteem. For some men this stress, combined with being at home for longer hours, sometimes alone with teens, and sometimes combined with alcohol, leads to sexual abuse.

Extended unemployment may lead to sexual assault outside the family for a variety of reasons. Teens may turn to outside activities to get out of a household atmosphere which is tense and frightening. They may feel the pinch of less money and may be more vulnerable to offers of jobs, or money, which sometimes turn out to be sexual abuse ploys.

Parents may exercise less limit setting due to their own fatigue and stress, and there may be changed or additional unsupervised hours if the other spouse finds a job to

supplement the family income.
  To minimize these effects:

- Talk to the teens about the effect the changed
  employment situation may have on the family.
- Set specific times for the family to be together
  and discuss problems which seem to be coming up
  as a result.
- Avoid any atmosphere of secrecy.
- Involve teens in concrete ways they can help the
  family.
- Talk about the extra stress on the unemployed
  person, but be clear that does not excuse any
  behavior other than a little extra grouchiness.

Cycles of Abuse

Families not only have a role in teen vulnerability but in
changing the cycle of abuse. A commonly accepted notion is
that children who are abused grow up and abuse others.
  Another family pattern which may contribute to teens
committing sexual assaults is that of high expectations of
success combined with little family communication and
affection. Perhaps many would call that "emotional abuse."
Treatment programs focus on:
  ...Gaining family participation and communication,
    especially about sexual values and relationships.
  ...Providing clear limits on aggressive behavior
    while providing new methods for handling
    frustration.
  ...Developing social skills to lower the teens'
    sense of powerlessness.

Perhaps the question we need to ask is why some men don't rape. Even men who agree with some ''rape attitudes'' are unwilling to use force or coercion themselves. Cycles of abuse can be broken. Overcoming shame and secrecy, joining with others to talk, and involving children and teens in problem solving can decrease further victimization.

Chapter 12

Recovery:

Responding If Your Teen Is Assaulted

Although this book is about prevention, in no way is it intended to mean that parents or teens are to blame if a sexual assault does occur.

Teens who have been assaulted have better chances for good recovery with support and help from their families. One of the goals of talking about aquaintance rape and sexual exploitation is to increase the likelihood that teens will tell their parents in the event of an assault. They are more likely to tell if they know their parents aren't going to blame them. Teens usually tell friends rather than parents because of their fear of upsetting their parents, loyalty to the offender, or the circumstances of the assault. They may have been breaking a rule and blame themselves.

The symptoms of an assault are similar to those associated with other teen troubles. A girl or boy who has been assaulted may:

...become withdrawn and head for her room upon return from school;

...suddenly find all his friends dull and stupid, saying things like, ''They don't know what the real world is like'';

...suddenly have trouble in school because of difficulties in concentration;

...become fearful, and want a night light or other comforts;
...want to move from a place where she has been happy;
...run away even though there has been no apparent
  problem.

The important feature of these symptoms is the *change* in
behavior. Some teens seem withdrawn or fearful by nature.
Others have difficulty in school for known reasons. These
behaviors are indicators only when they represent change.

Ideally teens would tell their parents about a sexual
assault. But for teens a rape feels like a failure of competence.
Victims often feel frightened and humiliated, and fear that if
they tell their parents their activities will be limited. Teens
who are assaulted when breaking a rule are afraid of getting
in trouble over the rule violation. Teens who are assaulted by
someone they know, or someone trusted by the family, are
afraid of being doubted and the resulting trouble.

Parents who do learn of an assault can help if they first
say:

"I believe you."

"I'm glad you told me."

"It's not your fault."

"I'll do my best to protect you."

SHORT TERM HURDLES

Decisions about: police, medical care and who
to tell.
Fears from: Having the world suddenly turn
unpredictable. Threats made by the offender.
Damage to your faith in humans.
Nightmares
Family stress from the crisis. Fathers often
threaten to "go out and shoot the guy," creating
more worry and fear.
Self-blame and recriminations.
Harassment at school for the teen.

Parents may be surprised to find their concerns are very
different from the victim's. Teens do not want their activities
limited. They may be ready to return to school, date, or go
back to a job before the parent is prepared for that. The teen
needs to reassert his or her competence in the world. Parents
want to provide even more protection than they have in the
past.

Yet, no matter how calm and collected the teen appears,
he or she is hurting. The trauma in a sexual assault often
seems to be the fear that he or she is going to die. The fear
has been described as like that experienced just before the
inevitable crash of an automobile accident. A rape victim
experiences over a prolonged time the surge of fear which
goes through the body in anticipation of the crash. How much
fear the victim feels after the rape varies. But even if the
assailant is known, the victim is likely to be fearful. Parents
can help by providing a nightlight, extra door checks, bars on
the windows, comforting after nightmares — whatever it
takes for the teen to begin to regain a sense of security.

ADOLESCENT CONCERNS	PARENTAL CONCERNS
Fear of bodily harm or for their lives	Concern for the child's safety (50%)
Shame, self-blame guilt	Blame the child (41%)
Anger at the assailant (45%)	Anger at the assailant (69%)
Fear of future sexual problems (21%)	Fear of future sexual problems (66%)

"Needs of Adolescent Rape Victims." From *Response*, May/June 1983

Medical Care

Parents can help the teen receive basic medical care for possible treatment of sexually transmitted disease, for pregnancy prevention, to provide reassurance that she or he is all right, or to collect evidence. Privacy and confidentiality between the doctor and teen are essential. The doctor must ask questions about specific details of the assault and about previous sexual intercourse for the tests and concern about pregnancy. The teen may not give honest answers with a parent present. The specifics of the sexual assault are one of the sources of trauma the teen may not share with the parent.

Many rapes involve other forms of sexual contact besides vaginal penetration. Many teens are ashamed of the other forced contact. After a medical exam or at a later time, the parent may be able to reduce the shame by saying,
"I know that often rapes involve other forms of

*sexual contact. He may have asked you to do some
things that seem really awful to you, and you are
afraid to tell me because somehow you are more
ashamed of them. But they aren't your fault and
you don't need to tell me. I just wanted you to
know I wouldn't be shocked, or think any less of
you. I'm just sad and angry that someone forced you
into anything."*

Outside the scope of this book are responses to
pregnancy. Families facing teen pregnancy usually benefit
from pregnancy counseling to help choose between the four
alternatives:
...Bearing the child and becoming a parent, married or
single.
...Bearing the child and giving it up for adoption.
...Bearing the child and having another family member
raise it.
...Abortion.

Police Reporting

Teens may want assistance in deciding about police
reporting and possible legal proceedings. (A medical exam is
a very important step in gathering legal evidence. Having the
exam done does not mean you have to go through with legal
proceedings.) The teen is the one who must make the report,
go to a lineup, and be prepared to testify, and therefore needs
to be in control of the final decision. Parents can assist and be
psychologically involved, but the teen must live with possible
repercussions at school or elsewhere. Teenagers may be cruel
to a rape victim, calling names and implying that the victim
was at fault. Male victims are probably even more reluctant to
make any formal report because of the fear of peer and parent
reaction.

*"As a rape crisis worker, I have certainly seen
many parents make the decision for a child or teen
about police reporting, in both directions, to report
and not to report. In fact sometimes they call the
police without consulting the child. I can't help
but disagree even though I know how hard decisions
are to make in a time of overwhelming crisis. The
parent doesn't go through the process of talking
to the police, the kid does. And often she may not
be telling the entire circumstances because she is
afraid of getting into further trouble. If the parent
calls the police, then she is doubly frightened of
being found out. Sexual offenders frequently take
advantage of teenagers' desire to experiment with
forbidden things — alcohol, drugs, and so on —
and then kids think they deserve what happened,
because they experimented."*

Legal Proceedings

If legal proceedings take place, parents can continue to
be helpful, for instance by keeping procedures straight and
asking for further information. Although procedures vary
from jurisdiction to jurisdiction, the following brief
description outlines what may take place. This information is
intended as a very general guide. Some police or courts may
respond better than indicated, others not as well:
• The police can take a report, and investigate a rape.
• They may not believe a teenager, and sometimes may show
that disbelief. Police are usually very sympathetic when the
circumstances of the assault involves no rule breaking on the
part of the teen. They have enough experience with troubled
teens however, that they tend to be suspicious of other
circumstances.

- Police in most jurisdictions cannot offer protection from the offender. In small towns or cities they may be able to provide some extra surveillance.
- Usually the first officer contacted takes a preliminary report. A detective later becomes involved to take a much more extensive report. This can be grueling for the teen, because it involves telling about the entire assault, in detail.
- The next step is the decision about whether or not the courts are going to pursue criminal charges. The procedure for making that decision varies. Teens are at a disadvantage in that process because the considerations are whether or not the case looks like it can be won, and how credible the victim is. Teens are seen as less credible in many cases. Past sexual history may be an issue, despite efforts to keep it out of the courts. Teens who are sexually active are less likely to be believed about a rape, especially an acquaintance rape. Because rape and child sexual abuse sometimes occur in the context of risk taking or breaking a rule, the victim is less credible to the authorities.

Civil Suit

Recently more people have been pursuing the option of a civil suit. The civil system operates with a different burden of proof: a ''preponderance'' of evidence rather than ''beyond a shadow of a doubt.'' In addition, because the attorney has been hired by the victim and/or family, the attorney is pursuing those clients' interests, rather than the interests of the state. The issue becomes one of personal injury rather than criminal behavior. Either the offender or a third party may be sued. Some families may want to consider this possibility.

Religious Crisis

Religious concerns may further complicate recovery. For teens, as for adults, the "lack of protection" from God may precipitate a crisis in faith. People in the religious community who are unfamilar with rape may complicate this further by placing blame on the victim. Fortunately, many religious communities are learning about sexual assault and how to help victims regain their faith and place in the community. The Center for the Prevention of Sexual and Domestic Violence (1914 N. 34th, Suite 205, Seattle, WA 98103, 206-634-1903) provides education and training for religious communities.

Parents can assist in the resolution of a possible crisis in religious faith. They should not be shocked or condemning of the teen's reaction, but help her or him find a sympathetic ear to help resolve the crisis.

Emotional Comfort

Typically in acquaintance rape or sexual exploitation the person who committed the assault continues to be around, without any legal action. Parents need to deal with their own anger about the hurt to their child and the lack of any punishment of the offender, without directing it at their child. The teen may be frightened, humiliated and uncertain about how to behave around the offender, who may even call for another date.

Parents can help by confirming their teen's perception of the assault. Teens may begin to feel they have overreacted. Parents can confirm that it is hurtful to be forced, and say, "That isn't what sex is about any more than being force fed is what eating is about."

Both parents and teens need help with the "If onlys":

"If only I hadn't let her go…"
"If only he hadn't been hitching a ride with
someone he barely knew…"
"If only I hadn't gone to that party…"

The "If onlys" can help parents and teens feel more in control by making it seem the assault could have been avoided, but the reality is that people take chances all the time, and not always is there someone standing by to take advantage of the situation and victimize the risk taker. Every teenager takes risks. Being raped is not a "risk" teens think they are taking.

If the situation involved any behavior the teen might feel guilty about, parents can reassure that everyone makes mistakes, but in this case the offender is at fault for taking advantage of the situation, and using force, pressure, deception, trickery. Self-blame and recriminations are part of the recovery process. Being able to blame oneself allows time to begin to deal with the unpredictability of the humans in the world. It is helpful for parents to talk about how the teen can feel safe in the future, to ask what he or she would like to do to feel more secure, and to continue to express that it was not the teen's fault.

Reassure the teen through appropriate touching and words that he or she is still loved and valued as much as ever. Teens may not want physical contact, but a parent can try touching while being alert for discomfort on the teen's part. Comfort with being touched will change. Parents need not take the rejection personally.

Parents can also say such things as,

> *"I admire your courage in facing this guy every day at school."*

> *"I have always liked your smile. It is good to see it again."*

*"I don't mind that you are sad sometimes, I know
it must be hard."*

Listen without offering advice, but respond to the
emotions. Remember the push-pull the teen is feeling,
wanting comforting, but not wanting to be thought incapable.
Parent and child may attempt to hide the effects of the crisis
from each other. The teen usually has a stake in being
competent and capable of handling anything on her own, the
parent has a stake in being strong enough to help the child
and not allow the child to see the parent in pain.

Psychological issues for a teen vary enormously but
several studies show there are effects even for a teen who
seems to be adjusting. Those effects may last as long as a
year, even two. Problems with areas such as self-worth,
trust, and fear are difficult to resolve. At adolescence, a rape
complicates the already difficult sexual development issues.
Parents can help find knowledgeable professional help to
speed the recovery process. A local rape crisis center may be
able to provide help directly or assist in locating it.

Parents need to recognize and seek help for their own
crisis caused by the teen's assault. Most parents experience a
sense of terrible failure if their teen is victimized. They often
have done everything they knew how to protect their child.
The feelings are normal; seeking help can allow parents to be
of more assistance to their child.

If all of this is dumped on a family when everything was
going full speed, something is going to change. It is going to
take some energy and time to recover, much as it would from
any other major trauma or accident. Things don't just go back
to normal, and what once was normal changes. Sometimes it
appears things are going fine, and suddenly a symptom
appears.

Overcoming Long Term Effects

Attention to the following areas can help parents feel less helpless in the recovery process.

• *Self-esteem* is damaged in a variety of ways. There are specific suggestions in Chapter 5. In addition parents can pay particular attention to overcoming any idea the teen may have that bad things only happen to bad people, so he or she must be bad. Discussions of sexual values and information may also be helpful to overcome the idea that the victim is "ruined" and therefore what he or she does sexually doesn't matter any more.

• *Academic and social difficulties at school* can cause otherwise competent students to fail and begin to doubt their abilities. Parents can assure teens that difficulty in concentrating is a natural symptom of any trauma. They will probably need to say that several times, as part of that symptom is not remembering reassurances like that.

The social difficulties are harder for parents to help with. What they can do is offer a sympathetic ear, and help the teen make decisions about sticking to the present situation or finding an alternative. Sometimes families move, or find another school for their teen if the situation becomes too difficult.

• *Wide mood swings and persistent depression* can be helped some with reminders to the teen that a slow recovery is not unexpected.

Depression is a common problem for victims. Sometimes talking out the feelings helps. Sometimes activity helps, but teens are too afraid to initiate it. Parents can encourage physical activities, and initiate family activities. Going to a movie with parents may not be what a teen has in mind, and they may have to be "dragged," but getting out in the world again, protected, is often needed. When someone is depressed, a bit more coaxing or pushing than usual might be needed.

Teens are dismayed when they think they are all right and then suddenly find themselves pitched back into the early crisis feelings. Teens frequently suffer from wide mood swings even without an assault. Sometimes the best a parent can do is to stay clear and remember that whatever the current mood, it may change shortly. A sexual assault may make those mood swings too wide and professional help is needed.

• *Phobias and fears* are often an outcome of a sexual assault. There are psychologists and other professional therapists who can help very directly with phobias. Parents can help the teen find physical and psychological ways to feel more secure. The difficulty is sympathizing with the teen's fear while not reinforcing the idea that there is reason to continue to be fearful.

• *Running away, alcohol, drug abuse, shift in friends, prostitution* are among the worst long term results. Sometimes despite parents' best efforts, a sexual assault triggers a cycle of troubled behavior too difficult for any family alone. Professional counseling and groups for parents of troubled teens can help parents find the least destructive ways to deal with these difficulties.

What About The Offender?

Not only do parents deal with their own children, they face questions about what to do about the offender. Here is a story which illustrates both a success and the dilemma often facing a parent:

> *A child came home from soccer practice and told his mom that he didn't know what to think about his coach.*

He said that while the coach was demonstrating something, he reached between the kid's legs and felt his crotch. The boy was confused. The mother was glad he had told her, but wondered what to do next. Should she talk to other parents? Confront the coach herself? Talk to the association about the coach? She was spared deciding because the coach was apparently also encouraging the use of marijuana, so the association asked him to leave.

Often the dilemma isn't as easily solved. And of course this man is still in some neighborhood someplace.

A parent confronted with this kind of situation first needs to assess her or his own support. Nobody is going to admit touching a child inappropriately. With a teen particularly, there may be a counteraccusation of seductiveness. (Unfortunately teenage girls sometimes do act inappropriately around teachers. This creates a genuine dilemma for both teachers who fear the accusation of sexual assault and for the parents of teens who have been assaulted by a teacher but find the accusation dismissed.)

A parent planning any action about the offender needs support. If it isn't available from family and friends, it may be useful to call a local crisis line for support even though the incident isn't "rape."

One of the primary considerations is the child's well being. Is she going to suffer terribly if the incident becomes known? Does the teen want to handle the situation on her own? As much as a parent may want to be sure that person never has a chance to touch a child inappropriately again, the older child's wishes should be considered to avoid re-victimization and cutting off communication.

Whenever possible, bring help in on your side in the form of some authority. Ask someone else to be there if you plan to confront the offender. Plan what you want from the offender. Don't expect an apology. Maybe you simply want him to know that you and others know what he is doing, and that he cannot operate in secrecy anymore. *If you make a threat, be sure it is a threat you can actually follow through on.* Don't threaten to get someone fired if in fact grievance policies won't allow that, or if the person victimized may not be willing to be involved in any proceedings.

> *"At one of the community colleges, there is an instructor who consistently touches students inappropriately during the course of instruction. He reaches around them to demonstrate something, then brushes their breasts. He has been involved in undocumentable incidents of greater violence as well. As a result some students have left school. He is still there because the embarrassment and humiliation are too much for the young women he is victimizing to want to testify in the proceedings necessary to fire the instructor."*

Advice From The Mother Of A Rape Victim

Parents of rape victims should get counseling for themselves. You need a professional support system *in addition* to friends and family members. The crisis and the events following reach out "like an octopus" to other family members, so it is very helpful to have someone outside to help put issues into perspective.

Be careful of your friends. Reach out to those who can cry and grieve with you just as they would if your child had been hurt in an automobile accident. Avoid those with the pat answers, especially those who tell you to "keep your chin up" or to "put it behind you," before it is time. The person who wants you to put it behind you is probably someone who doesn't handle emotional crises very well. This may be someone who projects a very strong image, giving the advice more power, but it is just an illusion of strength. It takes strength to grieve and deal with the pain.

The rape of a child, even a grown child, is devastating to the parent. Shock and grieving is normal. If your friends tell you to be strong and you listen and can't do it, it is easy to feel there is something wrong with you, instead of realizing it is poor advice. Professional counseling can help you sort out your expectations of yourself and help you set realistic goals toward recovery.

You may feel that as the parent you must hold together for your child's sake. A counselor can help in two ways. First, if you have an outside outlet for your own hurt and anger, you are going to be better able to cope when it is necessary for your child. Second, a counselor can help you decide how and what emotions to share with your child.

A counselor may be essential for preserving a marriage as well. Coping styles differ greatly and severe differences in coping with the rape of a child can precipitate a marital crisis in which unnecessary severe or permanent damage to the relationship results.

Most of us run full speed ahead in our everyday lives, and all of us have problems with which we are already dealing when a rape occurs. We can't just drop everything else and deal only with the rape. The rape may be an overload. A counselor can help sort the essentials from the not as essential and help set the priorities for the recovery period.

Professionals can help you overcome the sense of isolation which can sometimes occur if you chose the wrong person to talk to. The "stiff upper lip" approach leads to rigidness and isolation. Others don't know what your pain is, so they can't help and also can't get close to you to lend support.

Ideally there would be other parents to talk to, who have experienced the indescribable anger and pain and can say so. Others willing to share how they cope with it can save you some deadends. Someone who can say, "Of course you are hurting and it isn't going to just go away," can help you acknowledge the pain. It hurts when your daughter or son leaves the house and a stranger returns. Trading ideas with others about how to handle the practical problems — "Do you wake up a child having a nightmare, or let her or him sleep?" "Do you tell family members or keep it a secret?" — can at least reduce the sense of being all alone.

Surround yourself with friends who will cry with you; people who can be called at 2:00 a.m., when you have comforted your child through another screaming nightmare and can't go to sleep because of your own pain and anger. Seek out those friends who aren't afraid of your pain, and who will be honest with you: "Aren't you drinking more than you did?" "Are you still seeing your counselor?...What do you mean you didn't have time this week?" You need someone willing to tell you that time alone won't heal this pain, but it will heal.

You'll know recovery has occurred when you:

...no longer check each man on the street wondering if "that's him."
...can answer the telephone without jumping.
...feel sad or numb only occasionally about your loss.
...no longer feel overwhelming anger.
...can allow your child to take risks without feeling panicked.

...can have fun without feeling guilty.

...have resolved any spiritual crisis created by
    the assault.

...have regained the sense of having some control
    over your life.

...have resolved your feelings of failure as a parent,
    accepting that no parent can protect a child from all
    risks.

This process will probably take a minimum of six months, and may go on over the course of a year or longer. Recovery is a process of gradual lessening of symptoms. Recurring sadness or anger is natural and happens less often as recovery progresses.

Life Without Rape

Caren Adams

Today is one of those beautiful, sparkling fall days with warmth and coolness in the air. As I jogged I thought about what a beautiful day it was and the fact that so few people were out. When I got back to my car, I felt odd and self-conscious about being out there and I wondered what was the matter. Then I realized, I am a woman alone, moving around, out in the world. It (it being rape) is always on my mind when I run, at least peripherally. I check every car as it passes to see who is in it, to be sure that it is not going to hit me, and so that I will recognize it if it passes me again or if it is a car which passes me often. When someone, or a set of circumstances makes my danger seem particularly high, I start thinking about my escape routes, and actions, and on days when it gets really bad, I start planning my post assault activities.

But I think now of how our lives would be different if there were no rape.

To be able to walk, run or simply stroll on a lovely day like this, say hello to your neighbors and nod at whomever you liked without worrying about who might get the wrong idea. To be able to move about the house, letting animals, fresh breezes, children or whomever in and out without checking to be sure the doors are locked.

To be able to dress on warm summer days without worrying about how someone else is going to view what you have on.

To be able to go out at night, alone.

To be a parent and not fear for your daughter every time she goes out alone, or with a new date, or to a party where you don't know everyone, or where you do know everyone and you don't trust some of them. To be able to raise a girl or boy without being afraid that someone is going to sexually abuse him or her.

To be able to be friendly to men we like. How much friendlier might we be if we weren't being careful that "someone might get the wrong idea."

To be able to move about without the second thoughts and evaluations of relative risk.

To not have to take precautions which you know aren't even that likely to help.

To be raised without that cloud over your head. Who might we be and how different might our relationships with men be, and with women and with the world.

Surely we would fear less. No, I don't live my life in a cage. But I still pay a price, as we all do, and I know no way to stop paying.

Resources

FOR TEENAGERS

Top Secret: Sexual Assault Information For Teenagers Only, by Jennifer Fay and Billie Jo Flerchinger. Available from King County Rape Relief, 305 South 43rd, Renton, WA (206-226-5062). Excellent companion to this book. This popular 32 page booklet presents information about incest, date rape, offenders, self-protection, and how to help a friend who's been assaulted. Its format is lively and engaging — the kind of booklet that can be left on the coffee table to be "found" by teens.

Did You Hear What Happened To Andrea?, by Gloria D. Miklowitz. New York: Delacorte, 1979. Fictional story of a teenage girl who is raped by a stranger. Good description of her reactions, and those of her boyfriend and her family.

Dear Elizabeth, by Gene Mackey and Helen Swan. Available from the Children's Institute of Kansas City, 9412 High Drive, Leawood, KS 66206 (913-341-7006). Fictional diary of an adolescent victim of incest. Can provide useful insights into the problem of incest for teens.

FOR TEACHERS AND GROUP LEADERS

"Top Secret Teaching Guide," by Jennifer Fay and Billie Jo Flerchinger. Available from King County Rape Relief. A discussion guide for using *Top Secret* in the classroom or with a group of teens. Concise and simple to use.

"No Easy Answers Curriculum," by Cordelia Anderson, Illusion Theater, 304 Washington Ave., No., Minneapolis, MN 55401 (612-339-4944). 200 page sexual abuse prevention program for junior and senior high school students. Combines sexuality education with abuse prevention. Play "No Easy Answers" also available on videotape.

"Personal Safety And Decision Making," by Ann Downer. Committee For Children, P.O. Box 51049, Seattle, WA 98115 (206-522-5834). Lessons, activities, and background information for teachers on sexual abuse and exploitation for grades 7-9. Also videotape, "Straight Talk About The Streets And Sexual Exploitation."

"Source Book For Educators: Sexual Assault Prevention For Adolescents," by Susan De Alcorn. Available from Pierce County Rape Relief, Allenmore Medical Center, 19th and Union, Tacoma, WA 98405 (206-627-1135). 300 page collection of resources, background information, and lesson plans for sexual assault prevention. Includes teacher's guide. Geared to Washington state.

"Self-Protection: A Curriculum For The Developmentally Disabled," by Ellen Ryerson. Available from C.H.E.F., 20832 Pacific Highway South, Seattle, WA 98188 (206-824-2907). Level Two kit for junior and senior high, ages 12-19. Audio tapes, pictures, stories, and slide shows.

"Sexual Abuse Prevention, A Study For Teenagers," by Marie M. Fortune. United Church Press, 132 West 31 Street, New York, NY 10001. Particularly valuable for religious youth groups. Provides discussion guide covering abuse, self-protection skills, confusing touch, advertising messages.

FILMS

"Beyond Rape: Seeking An End To Sexual Assault," MTI Teleprograms, Inc., 3710 Commercial Ave., Northbrook, IL 60062 (1-800-323-5343). 28 minutes, high school audience or adult. 16 mm film or video available. A general approach to the problem of sexual violence and why it happens with a focus on prevention. Examines attitudes that contribute to rape. Explores feelings of victims without overwhelming the audience.

"Acquaintance Rape Prevention Series," O.D.N. Productions, Inc., 74 Varick Street, Suite 304, New York, NY 10013 (212-431-8923). (Also available from MTI Teleprograms.) Four-part film series, each about 10 minutes, including discussion guide, fact sheets, posters. Junior high and high school. Best used with an experienced discussion leader.

"Killing Us Softly, A Film About Media Images Of Women," 16 mm color film, 29 minutes. Cambridge Documentary Films, P.O. Box 385, Cambridge, MA 02139 (617-354-3677). Explores images of women as portrayed in advertising and other media. For high school students or adults. A series of magazine ads point out the sex role stereotyping inherent in their messages: women should be dominated; women look up to a man who overpowers them; hurting women is part of being a man.

"Child Sexual Abuse: What Your Children Should Know," Indiana University Audiovisual Dept., Bloomington, IN 47405, (812-335-8087). Videotapes of a five-part series by the Public Broadcasting System on preventing sexual abuse of teenagers and children. One segment is aimed at teachers and parents and includes general information about offenders and victims. Introduced by Mike Farrell of "M*A*S*H," the series includes two segments aimed directly at teen audiences.

"Aware And Not Afraid," Migima Designs, P.O. Box 70064, Eugene, OR 97401 (503-726-5442). 20 minute videotape. Five teens discuss frightening situations and how they successfully escaped them.

"Out Of The Trap," The Bridgework Theater, Inc., 133 East Lincoln Ave., Suite 3, Goshen, IN 46526, (219-534-1085). For junior and senior high school students, this 45 minute videotape of the play demonstrates situations of potential sexual abuse. Has accompanying guidebook.

If you have benefited from reading this book, you may be interested in other "titles with Impact." Impact Publishers is a small, independent company which publishes works on personal growth, relationships, assertiveness, parenting, and communities. For a free catalog, please write to Impact Publishers, Inc., Post Office Box 1094, San Luis Obispo, California 93406.